THE FEMALE HAND

Shows how women in particular can use the art of hand analysis
to analyse themselves, their loved ones and their associates; and
reveals how this knowledge can help them to direct and shape
their own lives as they choose.

By the same author
HOW TO READ HANDS

THE FEMALE HAND

PALMISTRY FOR TODAY'S WOMAN

by

LORI REID

With an introduction by Dr F.J.M. Reid
and fashion designs by Grace Crivellaro

THE AQUARIAN PRESS
Wellingborough, Northamptonshire

First published 1986

British Library Cataloguing in Publication Data

Reid, Lori
  The female hand
  1. Palmistry
  I. Title
  133.6   BF921

  ISBN 0-85030-516-0

The Aquarian Press is part of the Thorsons Publishing Group

Printed and Bound in Great Britain by
Whitstable Litho Ltd., Whitstable, Kent

To Lina
the most loving of mothers

ACKNOWLEDGEMENTS

My grateful thanks go to all those who have kindly permitted me to reproduce their hand prints.

CONTENTS

INTRODUCTION –
IS WOMAN MAN-
MADE?

Common sense tells us that women and men differ so obviously in appearance, in anatomy and bodily function, that the fact that they are species apart is beyond question. Yet it is the social meanings that we attach to these differences, the beliefs that we hold about their origins, and their hidden implications for our attitudes and behaviour towards our own and the opposite sex, that shape our views about the possibility for personal growth and change of individual men and women in our society. It is here that common sense falters; for many women and men it is self-evident that they are born to be different, physically and mentally, that these differences are a matter of reproductive function and are an immutable part of the natural order of things, and that our social world simply mirrors these contrasting biological destinies. But the last half-century has seen the appearance of quite a different brand of common-sense reasoning that points to equally obvious differences in the way male and female children are taught to dress, play, think and act in ways fitting to their sex and position in society, are channelled into suitable subjects at school and appropriate occupations in their working lives, and are taught to style themselves on the idealized images of femininity and masculinity purveyed by 'man-made' magazine and television advertisements.

Both brands of common sense start from the same physical facts about the sexes but reach starkly different conclusions about the meaning to be attached to these facts. Yet in one important respect, both views act as a straitjacket to personal growth and self-determination. For the woman or man faced with social rules which seem so rigidly to define what it is to be a 'feminine' woman or a 'masculine' man, the obstacles to any attempt to change one's career, marital or parental relationships, emotional attachments, or life-style may be as insurmountable as if one were faced with an immutable biological fact.

BIOLOGICAL PROGRAMMES AND CLOCKS

Whether a human being develops male or female physical characteristics is a lottery at the exact moment of conception. All normal human cells contain twenty-three pairs of strips of genetic material called chromosomes, one chromosome in each pair deriving from the sperm cell of the father and one from the ovum of the mother. It is the twenty-third pair, the sex chromosomes, that sets the biological clock running, and begins to differentiate male from female development: if one of these is a 'Y' chromosome the foetus develops male character-istics. Only males carry a 'Y' chromosome, and therefore a person's biological sex is always determined by his or her father. Whilst the 'Y' chromosome carries little genetic information, its presence occasionally allows genetic instructions carried on the 'X' chromosome derived from the mother to be expressed during the development of the individual. There are about seventy known genetic instructions on this 'X' chromosome, of which many are pathological (such as haemophilia) and only appear in combination with a 'Y' chromosome. As a result, females often act as unwitting carriers of disorders to which only their male offspring fall victim.

The presence of a 'Y' chromosome resets the biological clock and has a single effect on the developing human embryo. In the seventh week after conception, it triggers the cells forming into embryonic sex organs to develop as testes and secrete the male sex hormone, testosterone: in its absence, these cells develop into ovaries and proceed to secrete the female sex hormones, oestrogen and progesterone. From that moment on, the development of the physical sex of the foetus is entirely determined by these hormones. Because every human embryo will develop as a female unless its biological clock is reset by the presence of a 'Y' chromosome, it has occasionally been suggested that the female is the basic human form, the 'default option', whilst the male is a 'late addition' to the species.

Whatever the evolutionary order of precedence of male and female, it is clear that there can be no possibility of a human infant being born neutral or asexual. However, it is possible for the development process to go wrong, for infants occasionally to be born with ambiguous external genitalia or with genitals that are at odds with internal sexual organs. Often in these cases it is an inherited hormonal imbalance that is responsible. One such condition causes genetically female babies to be born with male genitals as a result of an excess of male sex hormones produced during foetal development. Although surgically corrected at birth, these girls have therefore been exposed to the masculinizing effects of male hormones and do tend to show more 'tomboyish' behaviour as they mature, although this effect is quite slight when compared with the wide variation in the behaviour of normal boys and girls of the same age.

The conclusion that hormonal levels and physical sex characteristics can have relatively minor effects on the development of a person's sense of identity as male or female is corroborated by a number of other facts. Differences in the levels of sex hormones produced by boys and girls before puberty appear to be far too slight to be responsible for the speed and depth with which their gender identities develop during childhood. Several cases have been reported of genetically male or female children tragically suffering surgical accidents or hormonal abnormalities who have been successful in developing identities as members of the opposite sex. Even fully developed adults can reverse their gender identities with the aid of surgery, as recent sex-change cases attest. Clearly, our physical form does not necessarily bind us to a private sense of ourselves as immutably male or female.

Nevertheless, the normal body is reminded of its genetic sexual programming with the onset of puberty and the massive increase in the production of sex hormones and the bodily changes that signal sexual maturity. Interestingly, both sexes secrete male and female sex hormones, though in different proportions, and both are required for normal development at puberty. Although evidence is beginning to emerge that adult males also undergo cyclical changes in hormonal levels – a fact which must challenge the widespread belief in the hormonal stability of men compared with women – the regular and dramatic increases and decreases in the levels of oestrogen and progesterone associated with the female menstrual cycle are often alleged to be responsible for emotional 'moodiness' and behavioural instability in women. Yet there is no evidence that women's work performance is impair-ed during the premenstrual or menstrual phases of their cycles.

Cyclic variations in mood are, however, reported regularly: but learned social attitudes towards menstruation, the widespread belief in the existence of the premenstrual syndrome by both men and women, and the enormous variation amongst women in symptoms experienced during menstru-ation cloud this issue. Certainly, pregnancy, childbirth and the menopause are periods in a woman's life when hormonal levels suddenly alter, but even here the relationships that may exist between hormonal levels on the one hand and feelings, behaviour and symptom-clusters like 'post-partum depression' and 'premenstrual tension' on the other are complicated by the effects of socially learned beliefs and attitudes which surround these changes in a woman's reproductive life, many of which are known to be more important determinants of emotions than are hormonal levels.

INTRODUCTION

ABILITY, ACHIEVEMENT AND AGGRESSION

If women are the 'weaker sex', the vital statistics for male and female life expectancies in this country do not fit well with this preconception. Although adult males are typically stronger physically, they are constitutionally the more vulnerable: figures for England and Wales in the early part of the last decade show that although more boys than girls were conceived and born, at every age male mortality exceeded that of females. For the most part, this was due to the greater susceptibility of males to diseases in infancy and to bronchitis, emphysema, heart disease and lung cancer in later life: but it was also the case that occupational and motor accidents, although statistically rarer than other causes of death, claimed more male than female lives. Women, therefore, form the numerical majority in this country, and there are many lonely women over the age of sixty-five.

Many of the popular stereotypes about men and women are based on the belief that they think in different ways, and this has often been used to justify preconceptions about the suitability of men and women to different occupations and professions. It is now known that the sexes do have different psychological strengths and weaknesses, but the number and the size of the differences is far smaller than these stereotypes would have us believe. Women are more socially sensitive, more attuned to nonverbal social messages, and form more lasting and intimate relationships than do men, but it is likely that these social skills are a product of the kinds of social relationships that women are expected and encouraged to establish in our society. It is possible that these skills may partly depend on their superior verbal abilities but even here research on adults and children in this country is at odds with findings elsewhere, particularly in the United States: whilst American girls appear to have the edge over boys by the age of ten and maintain this lead throughout their adolescence, research with English schoolchildren and adults has not always concluded likewise.

It is, however, often claimed that boys show greater

mathematical prowess, ability to visualize spatial arrangements and excel on manipulative problems, inherently suiting them to the scientific and technological professions, whilst women, with their heightened verbal skills, are more suited to secretarial work. It is true that adolescent boys and male adults show some superiority in solving visual and spatial problems. Although there is some evidence that in boys the right hemispere of the brain – that part of the brain believed to be linked to spatial reasoning – develops earlier and becomes more specialized than that of girls, it is also the case that this aspect of brain development is complete well before differences between the sexes in spatial thinking abilities become apparent, and that children of both sexes encouraged to play with manipulative toys (such as Lego or Meccano) and to take an interest in model-making and woodwork perform better than other children on tests of spatial ability. It therefore seems unlikely that a simple link exists between the 'natural' development of the brain in boys and girls and their suitability for different occupations in later life: the attitudes of their parents towards the forms of play and childhood activities that they consider appropriate to the two sexes may play an important part in hastening or impeding the development of specific functions within the brain and hence thinking abilities and skills.

Despite achieving nearly comparable standards in A-level, O-level and CSE grades, women in Britain are nonetheless outnumbered two to one by men on degree courses, and are four times more likely to train as teachers or nurses and six times more likely to enter a clerical occupation. The employment pattern in this country is clear-cut – many times the number of men compared with women enter higher-status and potentially better-paid jobs, receive occupational training and look forward to good promotion prospects. Even the advent of labour-saving computer technology is unlikely to benefit women: it is their jobs which will be lost as a result of office automation, and it is probable that those women who stay in employment will find themselves allotted tedious and repetitive tasks in the computerized office. Popular stereotypes about what is men's work and what is women's work have an undeniable impact on girls' choice of subjects at school, on beliefs about women's reliability and dependability as employees, and on inferences about unfeminine aspects of the personalities of successful women. It is hardly surprising, therefore, that psychologists have found that men and women develop quite different expectations and aspirations about their working and family lives.

It was thought until fairly recently that so powerful were these socially-transmitted beliefs that as well as not expecting to achieve great things in their lives, women also acquired an outright fear of success: because of its association with masculine striving and achievement, success for a woman was thought to be linked to fears about losing friends and becoming unfeminine and sexually unattractive. It is now evident, however, that whilst these fears accurately reflect men's social attitudes, women's lower occupational status is the direct result of reduced opportunity and lowered expectations rather than a deep-seated psychological aversion to succeeding in a man's world.

Because of inequalities in occupational and social opportunity, it should come as no surprise that men and women differ in the extent to which they can exert power and the kinds of power that they use. Men more frequently wield power openly and directly in social relationships, whereas women become accustomed to exerting influence through indirect and subtle manipulation. Yet there is no evidence that these styles of power are built into and differentiate the sexes. Women who are successful and occupy positions of legitimate authority in our society quite happily use direct forms of power. In the absence of status or authority, however, nonverbal gestures and signals signifying dominance regularly appear in male social behaviour, whilst submissive and compliant nonverbal signals are manifested in female nonverbal behaviour.

But women can be just as assertive and forceful and often as physically aggressive and violent as men, although statistics on violent crime, wife and child battering, and rape as well as the numerous studies of physical and verbal aggression in children and adults – all show that it is men who are more predisposed to violent acts in our society than are women. Claims that this predisposition is triggered by an overproduction of the male sex hormone, testosterone, do not reflect the whole picture: patterns of aggressive behaviour are first observed in boys at the age of three, well before the dramatic increase in testosterone levels at puberty. Social attitudes towards aggression in girls and boys – where physical violence is usually strongly disapproved of in girls and where boys are encouraged to 'stick up for and look after themselves' – seem to predispose boys far more than girls to view physical force as the answer to conflicts and difficulties in social relationships. The fact that husbands who were themselves beaten as children or who witnessed their fathers beating their mothers are more likely to beat their wives, and the finding that even women who observe their parents being violent are more likely to use physical violence within the family, seem to confirm that physical violence is a learned strategy for coping with difficulties in social relationships.

MARRIAGE, THE FAMILY AND SEX

Although men and women are, in our society, led to expect personal fulfilment in marriage and parenthood, the impact of these events differs between the sexes. Women, and in particular married women, are twice as likely to suffer from depression and anxiety than are married or single men. Some studies have linked these disorders to specific stages and events during marriage and parenthood, and to the burden of caring for young children at home in particular. The loss of employment and of relationships outside the small family circle, and a house full of young children are known to be risk factors associated with clinical depression in women. Being at work protects women from the full impact of marriage: whilst men's health improves as a result of marriage, women are on the whole healthier living on their own.

Some think that the drudgery and tedium of being

a wife and mother has declined with the advent of household gadgets and convenience foods. For many women, however, marriage brings with it feelings of reduced control, increased dependency and helplessness and a loss of meaning in their lives. Children may fill this vacuum, but once they themselves marry and leave home, baking bread and cultivating a vegetable garden may, for the housewife, become psychologically necessary activities rather than the economic necessities they once were.

Once the family has been stripped of most of its functions other than reproduction and child-rearing, it becomes all too easy to explain its continued existence by reference to biological programming. One influential theory claims that human evolution has come to predispose men and women to learn different life skills with differential ease. Although men can learn how to look after children, this theory suggests that they will find this far more difficult to do than women because they must overcome their biological tendencies not to be particularly interested in the very young. Fathering is socially learned whilst mothering has evolved over millions of years. Social attitudes may even reflect this predisposition: the father who assumes responsibility for the care of his home and children receives far less financial and psychological support than does the mother who seeks economic support outside the family.

If this were a biological fact, however, one would expect to find that young children would more readily establish stable, intimate and lasting attachments to their mothers than to their fathers. It is widely supposed that children suffer in later life if prolonged and intimate care is missing from early childhood: love and tenderness is presumed to be as important to the child's mental health as vitamins and proteins are to his or her physical health.

But does it matter which parent provides this love? The evidence at present indicates that, as far as healthy development is concerned, it does not matter. A pioneering study of newly born infants two decades ago showed that strong emotional attachments were often formed with more than one adult, that these attachments included fathers and grandfathers, and that occasionally bonds were formed with a single male adult.

Infants do not seem, therefore, to be pre-programmed to form unique bonds with their mothers. There is no reason, except for cultural and social assumptions about what they should undertake within the family, why men should not play a greater role in the care and upbringing of children. Indeed, most children's development and progress would follow quite a different course if their fathers were not to do so. In the typical Western family, each parent makes a different contribution to their childrens' development; the father by providing exciting physical play, especially after the first six to nine months of infancy, the mother physical care and verbal stimulation. This advantage of dual roles in play and stimulation of children is denied to one-parent families, in which the vast majority of children live with their mothers. Although financial hardship and difficult life conditions are often very severe for one-parent families, this varied play environment may be part of the reason why arithmetic ability, and possibly spatial and manipulative skills as well, are known to develop at a slower rate among children from fatherless families.

Not only is family life and parenthood imbued with socially-transmitted attitudes and expectations, but so too is sexual experience and behaviour. Men and women experience sexual satisfaction with similar bodily responses, although they obviously differ anatomically. Well-publicized surveys have shown this, and one would expect them to dispel mistaken notions about womens' limited sexual responsive-ness and the Victorian myth that it is in the natural order of things that women should endure but not enjoy sex and that satisfaction comes rarely if at all. Yet a double standard still exists: males are assumed to be naturally more highly sexed than women, to be the initiators and pursuers, whilst women coyly resist or reluctantly comply. Not only does this double standard induce women to mistrust men and their sexual motives, it puts men under great pressure to exhibit their masculinity by performing more than adequately as a sexual partner: often so severe is this pressure that an irrational fear of homosexuality, called homophobia, can result. Women, too, suffer from similar pressures: the emphasis on romantic attachment and love as the socially acceptable context for sexual feelings can lead them to overlook or deny messages from their own bodies. Recent studies have found that although both sexes show similar bodily responses to erotic stories, women often fail to recognize these bodily reactions unless the stories contain a romantic element or theme.

IMAGES OF FEMININITY

Few would argue with the claim that the modern media hold the key to political and cultural change. Advertising in particular has a powerful voice in communicating images of womanhood in present day society. Television, magazine and newspaper advertising not only reflects existing images of femininity, it reshapes and remoulds them too. Advertisers promote their products by exaggerating selected social attitudes towards femininity to which women and men of all ages are attracted and drawn. Yet many women wish to alter their family lives and personal relationships in ways which depart from these images, and it is often in the advertiser's interest to ignore or distort these trends.

A survey of advertisements broadcast by British commercial television in 1979 revealed that men and women are portrayed in very different ways. In 92 per cent of advertisements, men were presented as experts on the technical aspects of the product, typically by providing authoritative 'voice-overs', whilst women were shown as uninformed mothers, housewives, consumers whose choice of product could be completely decided by knowledgeable male advice. Television advertising fails to reflect even the most fundamental social facts about the place of women in modern British society. Although 41 per cent of all employees in Britain in 1979 were female, the fantasy world of television advertising represented working women in only 13 per cent of adverts.

A recently published analysis of British women's magazines reveals the kinds of hidden messages that are used by advertisers, messages that are often at odds with the picture of women as thinking individuals conveyed by the articles and features in the magazines themselves. Advertisements depicting women as mothers and wives in surroundings of idyllic domesticity, though on the decline, continue to imply that if the female reader's life is not as happy and harmonious as that portrayed, these short-comings can be instantly remedied by purchasing the products advertised. Apparently, a good wife has an obligation to stimulate her husband's interest and cheer him up when he gets home from work by presenting him with meals with 'man-appeal', or by looking as enticing as she can. More recently, advertisements have begun to capitalize on the image of the working mother on whom, however, the bulk of household chores continue to fall; oven-ready meals now deliver the dubious freedom to cook and care for home and family as well as pursue a working career.

The beauty and fashion ideal represented in many adverts requires 'today's woman' to compete through her appearance for the attention of her husband, lover or boss. Many advertisements for beauty products depict the modern women as more active than in the past, yet this activity often entails a laborious beautification process to transform her into a passive object to be looked at and admired, awaiting her man's initiative. As well as positive and desirable aspects of beauty, some advertisers exploit womens' fears and anxieties and cultivate envy and self-reproach: for example, the ugly scene of gossiping friends is among the advertiser's chief weapons to encourage women to seek treatment for unwanted facial hair.

But do the majority of women accept advertising's ideal of femininity? The editorial content of most magazines reflects a far more emancipated and self-sufficient image of the 'new woman' than that depicted in the advertisements they carry. Yet the dream business is far too clever to present a balanced and accurate picture of society as it is. As long as women continue to think of themselves as housewives, advertisers will continue to address them as housewives. Even when adverts depict the independent woman in a full-time career, she is portrayed as a busy, but feminine, career woman in a prestigious job quite out of character with the lot of the majority of Britain's working women.

The women's movement in Britain and the USA has, of course, attempted to change all this. Recognizing the powerful impact of 'man-made' images on women's beliefs and aspirations, women's groups have repeatedly lobbied organizations responsible for advertising standards, though with little observable success. Yet on the broader canvas of social life, these groups have achieved change, if not on the scale aspired to by radical feminists. Because working women are still under-paid, because so few attain positions of power and influence, because so many are the victims of male violence, it is easy to suppose that feminist aspirations are no more than an impossible dream. Yet from the suffragettes of the first two decades of this century to the radical feminism of the 1960s and the liberal feminism of the 1970s, the social pressures and constraints on womens' lives have been chipped away, fragment by fragment. But the wheels of equality grind exceedingly slow, and there is yet far to go.

This introduction began by posing common-sense views on the sexes as a riddle. This riddle can, however, be untangled (if not entirely solved) by accepting that common sense tells us something about the barriers we face in changing our lives, and the scope that might exist for personal fulfillment if these barriers can be overcome. It is not particularly fruitful to ask how much of our being male or female is to be attributed to our biological make-up, and how much it is due to the way in which social and cultural forces mould our identities. The 'how much?' approach depicts 'femaleness' and 'maleness' as a kind of recipe in which biological and social ingredients are added in different amounts to produce the finished product. Yet this approach obscures the fact that it is the interplay between biological, social, economic and political forces that shapes us as individuals. If instead we ask the question 'how?' – how does each of these factors act upon the others during development and at maturity – we may, as individual women and men, exert a measure of self-determination over our own actions and choose our own path, shaping the physical, the social and perhaps even the political worlds in which we live.

Dr F.J.M. Reid
September 1986

Chapter 1

HAND ANALYSIS FOR EVERYDAY USE

The Female Hand is aimed at women of all ages, of beliefs, of all political persuasions and of all walks of life. Whoever she is or whatever she is, a woman has to take on many, many different roles not only in the normal course of a day but indeed throughout her life. Daughter, wife, mother, lover, employee, businesswoman, cook, cleaner, nurse, housemaid, friend, confidante, teacher, seamstress, adviser – the list is endless. Some of these roles she carries off superbly well; some, alas, are abysmal failures. Hardly surprising, really, when you consider that these roles have often to be switched into and out of sometimes within seconds of each other. Successful role changes, then, require adaptability and ingenuity, gifts with which fortunately women seem to be blessed. But whether these gifts are inherent or acquired, however, is a moot point.

This book centres around the hypothesis that a woman, because of her position within the family, is really the nucleus, the prime mover, amidst her circle and that, as such, she has her finger on the pulse of life and is able to control and shape people and events around her. Because in most cases she is around the children more, she is usually the one who first notices their needs, their distress, their progress, the things that give them most pleasure or even the state of their health. Whether she has a career of her own or whether, for whatever reason, she is at home for the better part of the day, more often than not she is the one who deals with the running of the household, she is the one who has to interact with the plumber, with the painters and with the builders.

Whatever her marital status – single, married, divorced or widowed – she has to cope with all sorts of relationships that confront her throughout her life, all the time coming to terms with her own bodily changes through puberty, menstruation, pregnancy, giving birth, and the change of life. All these different stages bring with them their own problems, make their own demands, and require readjustment, acceptance and reorientation. And at every stage she is forced to re-evaluate herself, to acknowledge her new physical state and then to interpret it back into her life, into her relationships and into her family group.

All these different facets of our lives are marked out on our hands, rather like a road map, and with a little knowledge of the principles of hand analysis we are better able to choose the direction in which we wish to steer and in a sense to become 'street wise' about the course and running of our lives. A good interpretation of our hands can reveal much about our potential, our characters, our drives and motivation. What sort of lovers we are, what we think about our work, our friends and associates, how our childhoods have shaped and influenced our lives, past events and future possibilities are all marked there. Our state of mind and matters concerning our health and well-being are clearly shown together with any changes, be it connected with career, change of address or location or indeed any changes in our way of life. In fact, our hands are like mirrors of our very selves reflecting the types of people we are, with both our conscious and subconscious sides inextricably laid out for each of us to see.

To be able to use this information, then, must surely be an invaluable help to the smoother running of our lives. Once the basic concepts are learnt we can then begin to have a greater control not only of ourselves but also of the people and events around us. We no longer need to feel that we are puppets or the victims of our circumstances but that indeed we are able to forge our own destinies for ourselves. That is why this knowledge becomes so important particularly to women who need to be so many different people all rolled into one.

For the young girl who is just starting out in life a little understanding of the principles of hand analysis might help to give her confidence when confronting some of the new experiences life has in store for her. In situations such as interviews, interacting with her fellow workers, striking up new friendships or meeting boyfriends, a quick look at the respective hands of the people encountered would be enough for her to get a shrewd idea of the sort of behaviour or relationship the situation demands.

Hand analysis is invaluable to a mother when it comes to understanding her children and what makes them tick. It is particularly useful during those difficult adolescent years because, with a quick look at their heart lines, she can help to guide them through their emotional development. And then, when it comes to that tricky time of choosing options in the school curriculum, nothing is simpler than to look at their head lines and judge whether they are artistically, scientifically or practically orientated and thus encourage and advise them accordingly. The simple rule is: the straighter the head line, the more practical and scientific the mentality; the more curved the line, the more creative, artistic and imaginative the mind. Monitoring health, too, is another way of using hand analysis and so a mother can keep a watchful eye on her offspring, noting her children's susceptibilities to particular illnesses and, where possible, preventing those diseases from happening altogether.

For the woman whose household revolves around her, an understanding of hand analysis would certainly come in useful on many occasions. If, for instance, she has to negotiate with builders who are to install a new kitchen, a glance at their hands will instantly tell her which one will be painstaking with detail but will, therefore, spend months over it, or which one will be jolly quick and get the job done in a weekend, but perhaps may cut a few corners here and there in the process! In very general terms, long fingers equal slowness and patience with detail whilst short fingers are inspirational but quick. Empowered with this information, then, she will be able to choose between them with supreme confidence.

To the career-minded lady whose assessment of character is so important, merely looking at the hands of those around her can confirm her beliefs and expectations. Which colleague will be sympathetic to her aims, which one is quite ruthless and unprofessional, how best to interact with different superiors – all these questions can be answered by glancing at their respective hands. As an employer, to be able to analyse her employees in this efficient way must surely contribute to smoother working relations. Changes of jobs or even of careers are revealed in her hand and all she needs to do is carefully study her fate and life lines for any breaks or detours, apply the dating system in order to time the events, and she will then be able to make her decisions and lay her plans well in advance.

For wives and lovers the ability to read and compare their own hands with those of their partners must surely be a great advantage for this helps to fathom out the subtleties and complexities of their relationships. By comparing and contrasting the events recorded on the lines it is possible to gauge whether they will share similar experiences and indeed whether the two lives are likely to continue in parallel or not. The likelihood of offspring, changes of residence, of jobs, careers or life-styles, the possibility of redundancy, financial issues, emotional trauma, shared interests, happiness and fulfillment are all marked here to see.

That time in her life when a woman's children have grown up and flown the nest can be to some a relief but to most a devastating event. The demands grow fewer, the hours grow longer and the silence lingers. Those women who have a career, social commitments or many hobbies can easily fill their days and fall into a new and more relaxed routine. But for those who have devoted themselves solely to their families, who perhaps long ago gave up their career, and sometimes even their identities, it can be a time of crisis. This is where hand analysis can triumph.

Here it can be used to assess potential, to encourage the individual to develop some of those skills and talents that have been lying dormant for so long, to stimulate her into allowing her natural gifts to flourish and to concentrate these into hobbies, pastimes or perhaps to even start a business of her own. In this way she may come to realize that although her old life is coming to an end, she can look forward to a whole new life which is, in fact, just about to begin.

Chapter 2

FACING UP

This chapter sets out to establish your basic character according to the type of hand you possess. It is a time when you have to confront your own fundamental personality, when you can relish your virtues and delight in all your good qualities, but also admit to the not-so-good ones, to all your faults and foibles – in short, to find out 'which face suits you'.

When considering the actual shape of the hand traditional palmistry books talk about seven different types but, as very few hands conform exactly to type, I feel it is more sensible to treat the palm, fingers and thumbs separately and to analyse each independently of the others. The palm shapes can be simply broken down into the square, the conic, the spatulate and the psychic and these categories can also be applied to the fingers. In the traditional system the square hand, for instance, would be described with square fingers but the beauty of this new approach is that it is flexible and so allows an individual with a mixed hand to interpret each section discretely.

People have often remarked to me that one of their greatest difficulties is in working out which hand shape they actually possess and indeed this is not an easy task, especially for a beginner in hand analysis, or for the casual observer. This, I am sure, is due to the fact that most hands do not conform neatly to the pure types that are classically described but are confused with elements from several of the different categories – hence another good reason for analysing palms and digits separately. In the short term, the answer to this problem might be to take a print of the hand, measure it carefully on paper and compare it to the description provided for each type. Of course, the best way is simply to look at as many hands as possible and very soon experience will show how the different shapes do recur and eventually the categories fall automatically into place.

When analysing the hand in this way, however, it must always be remembered that each level of interpretation needs to be modified and refined by every other until a true picture is built up. In other words, subtle distinctions regarding the type of palm may be made when the indications of the fingers are taken into account and still further polishing will take place when information about the thumb is also added. In the ultimate analysis, it is the course and structure of the lines that put the final modifications to the whole picture.

PALM SHAPE

The square palm

The square palm (Figure 1a) is so called because when measured it is as long as it is broad, and the width at the wrist is the same as that at the base of the fingers.

This type is essentially the sign of a hard worker. Ladies with square palms will have masses of common sense, their feet are firmly planted on the ground and they are extremely practical in all aspects of life. This lady is strong and robust and she is always prepared to roll up her sleeves and get stuck in – no matter how dirty or arduous the task. She can work solidly and consistently, and if the job is tedious and repetitive she, of all the types, is more likely to be the one who stays at it until the bitter end. In fact, she can be described as truly a willing work-horse. In daily life she likes routine and gets rather upset if the normal pattern of her day is thrown out by unexpected events for, in general, she particularly finds it hard to adapt to changes. Mostly, she likes

Figure 1a

her life to run like clockwork and if she lacks somewhat in creative imagination she more than makes up for it in practical know-how.

She is basically an earthy type in her approach to life and even in her sense of humour. And, talking about earth, she is in her element in the great outdoors. Gardening, walking, communing with nature – these are the kinds of activities which suit her well.

Her views may be described as fairly conservative, especially so as she grows older, and she has a particularly strong sense of law and order. She loves tradition for this confirms her need for stability and purpose in life. And she may also show a strong materialistic streak as this, for her, provides the security she needs.

The conic palm

Figure 1b

Conic palms (Figure 1b) are narrow at the base, broaden out to accommodate a rounded percussion (outside edge of palm) and taper off again towards the fingertips. In its purest form the conic hand looks rather oval in shape.

Ladies with conic palms are very feminine and extremely creative. It is the bowed percussion which reveals their strong artistic flair and if the palm is accompanied by short fingers they can also be highly intuitive. Indeed, they are quick to pick up anything new for they are perceptive, with an insight that can be razor sharp. They are excellent at anything connected with organizational skills and prefer to plan projects and set ideas into motion rather than carrying out the tasks themselves, as impatience and inconsistency are some of their more negative qualities.

This palm type is always the mark of flexibility and adaptability. Ladies with the conic palm enjoy change and variety. They love to have several things on the boil at the same time, to be busily making plans, exchanging views and ideas and to be constantly one step ahead. Unlike the square type, a job or way of life which revolves around routine would completely stifle these ladies for whom the need to display their versatility in life is of the essence. Generally, they have a vast amount of enthusiasm and go through life with a cheerful optimism which makes them warm and approachable. They are attractive and often very sexy.

The spatulate palm

The spatulate palm has two distinct forms. The first, as illustrated in Figure 1c, is broad at the base and tapers up towards the fingers whilst the second, illustrated in Figure 1d, is narrow at the wrist, broadening out so that its greatest width is at the top just beneath the fingers. Whereas the conic is essentially a feminine hand type, the spatulate is more commonly found amongst men although some women do possess this shape, or at least, some elements of it.

In both cases, the spatulate palm denotes restless energy. It is the mark of the pioneer, the explorer, the inventor, the creator – this hand type loves excitement and the thrill of a challenge and is drawn, like a magnet, to adventure.

When the width is at the base it shows physical activity and people with this formation are often fond of sport. The power house of the body is represented by the basal part of the hand, within the bottom mounts just above the wrist so, if this part is large, it highlights physical strength and energy.

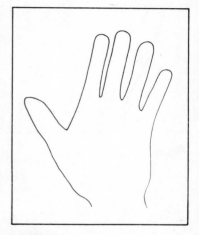

Figure 1c

If the width is found at the top of the palm, just below the fingers, it denotes mental energy, so a lady with this palm shape would have a very active mind. These people are highly imaginative and delight in generating ideas for they are excellent at invention or innovation but, quite unlike people with conic palms, they stick enthusiastically to their projects and see them through to the end.

The psychic palm

The psychic palm (Figure 1e) is long, lean and slender. It may have a slight development at the percussion but overall it is a graceful, elegant and beautiful hand.

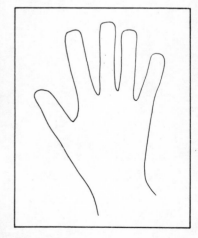

Figure 1d ·

Essentially, this marks an eye for the sensitive appreciation of artistic creation, of aesthetics, of poetry and of beauty. Anyone with a psychic palm

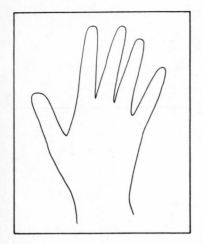

Figure 1e

will possess extremely refined tastes which may be considered quite exquisite. Although called psychic it does not necessarily follow that all these people have mediumistic powers but it does convey the idea of sensitivity and impressionability – indeed, they seem to be able to absorb the prevailing mood around themselves and so tend to be easily influenced.

Ladies with psychic palms almost live on a different plane with their heads in the clouds and their feet hardly touching the ground at all. In fact, they are not very realistic and quite the opposite to the sensible, earthy square types. Psychics are dreamy, moody, spiritual, highly idealistic people, not at all practical and often fretful and highly strung. For these reasons they need to be taught how to handle the practicalities of everyday life – or at least find a partner who will deal with all the mundane, materialistic issues required to keep body and soul together.

They prefer mainly indoor pursuits and, as they are usually urbane and very cultured, town or city life suits them far better than a rural existence. They are, just as their hand shape describes, elegant and graceful, often cool and sophisticated with an enigmatic quality which gives them an air of fascination and mystery.

THE FINGERS

Of course all these types will be modified by the shape, length and formation of the fingers. Pure types are those hands where the fingers match the palm perfectly so that square palms would be topped by square fingers, conic palms by conic fingers and so on. But as few hands can be classified as pure, special attention must be given to the nuances of character and personality that are highlighted by the digits.

The shape

Square fingers (Figure 2a) are, of course, the perfect complement to the square palm and where these are seen they would reinforce all the qualities represented by that type. If a majority of square fingers top a conic palm they would add a basic earthiness and bring a more methodical influence to an otherwise impatient nature. On a spatulate palm they could tone down that spirit of adventure so that caution and impulsiveness would be constantly in conflict. With a psychic palm square fingers would be very rarely found but if they were they would lock the imagination and clip the wings of those flights of fancy, bringing them crashing down to earth.

Conic fingers (Figure 2b) accompanying the conic palm would turn it into a pure type but if found with the square palm they would add adaptability, creativity and a lighter feminine side to that pragmatic nature. A majority of conic fingers on a spatulate palm would enhance the restlessness and need for adventure so that the realization of many solid and worthwhile ideas might be forsaken in the lure of a constant stream of new and exciting projects and experiences. These fingers would probably be an asset to the psychic palm for they would speed up reactions and bring a greater sense of worldly wisdom to an otherwise dreamy and unrealistic nature.

A majority of spatulate fingers (Figure 2c) would provide more imagination to the square hand and would make a good partnership. With the conic palm they would enhance the lively mind and provide a more methodical application of its ideas. With a psychic palm, it is debatable whether the combination would be beneficial or not because the get-up-and-go energy implied by the fingers contrasts markedly with the head-in-the-clouds nature denoted by the palm.

Psychic fingers (Figure 2d) on a square palm would add aesthetic and ethereal qualities thus lifting the whole personality from the purely earthy plain into the spiritual realm. With the conic palm they would enhance the intuition and inspiration. And together with spatulate palms they could bring deeper penetrative powers and insight into far-ranging concepts and ideas.

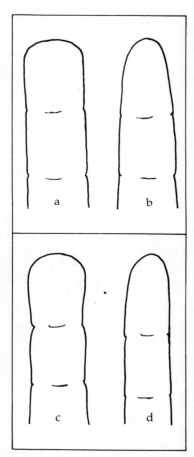

Figure 2

Finger length

Whether the fingers are short or long (Figure 3) is

35

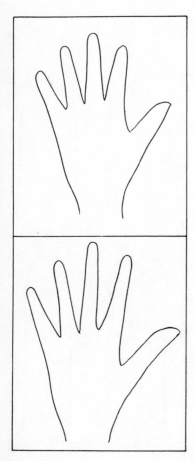

Figure 3

determined by comparing the middle, or Saturn, finger to the length of the palm. If the length of this digit, from its tip to the bottom joint crease, measures roughly three-quarters the length of the palm, it is considered as average. So, anything less than this would signify that the fingers are short, and equally, anything greater denotes long fingers.

Short fingers accompanying any of the palms tell of intuition and instinctive reaction. They always signify impatience with detail and with stupidity. They work fast, take things in at a glance and read between the lines. A lady with short fingers makes an excellent organizer for she has the ability to take an overall view of any situation, but don't ever expect her to dot the i's or cross the t's, for this sort of precision or punctiliousness of character is not in her nature.

Long fingers, however, are quite the opposite. These ladies can sit for long periods engrossed in meticulous detail, dealing with fine, elaborate work. They have great patience in anything requiring a careful, methodical approach but this makes them quite slow in their reactions and thought processes.

Whereas women with short fingers take an overall view of life, those with long fingers zoom in on the particular. For example, when a lady with short fingers visits a friend at home she will take in the colour scheme, the arrangement of the furniture, the view from the lounge and the overall feel of the house. She won't notice the stain on the carpet where the children spilt the cocoa, the crooked picture in the corner by the window, the jammy fingerprints on the doors, or the book shelf that's been propped up for months by a couple of bricks, waiting for someone to screw the bracket back in the wall. But a long-fingered lady would notice all these things – and more: the spode plate on the sideboard, the exquisite Indian miniature, the bargello cushion, the dust on the skirting boards, the torn wallpaper that's just peeping out from behind the curtains, three days' accumulation of empty milk bottles on the kitchen work-top, the ladder that's slowly creeping up her hostess's leg. And the new colour scheme? Oh, had they recently redecorated? – How funny, she hadn't noticed that!

The joints

There is a clear distinction, as illustrated in Figure 4, between hands with smooth fingers and those where the digits have markedly protuberant joints. Smooth fingers always reveal the quick thinker, the lady with inspirational ideas. Impressions are formed instantly and responses are fast.

But when the joints are prominent so that the outlines of the digits are quite bumpy, they are known as knotted or philosophical fingers. Ladies with these types of fingers are analytical, thoughtful, meditative and contemplative people. They take time to process information and so appear slow to respond and react. They do not rely on first impressions but carefully consider and study each problem or situation before they come to any conclusions.

When only the bottom joints are prominent and the rest of the finger is smooth, it tells of someone who needs a structured and ordered environment. Some ladies with these types of fingers can be compulsively houseproud whilst others, who may apparently seem untidy, nevertheless have such a neat, mentally-ordered system that they know exactly where everything is!

INDIVIDUAL FINGERS

Traditional palmistry has allocated mythological names to the fingers because, as each one represents certain principles, the classical allusion instantly captures the whole meaning in a form of shorthand jargon. For instance, some of the areas that are covered by the little finger include communications, science and literary skills and so consequently it is otherwise known as the Mercury finger because Mercury was the messenger of the gods and thus, in the one word, the whole idea of imparting information is conveyed. Figure 5 illustrates the names given to each finger.

The way the finger is held, whether it is straight, inclines to one side, over-short or longer than average, are important points to notice as each observation will add to the nuances of individual characteristics.

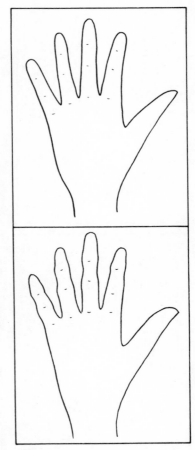

Figure 4

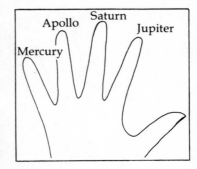

Figure 5

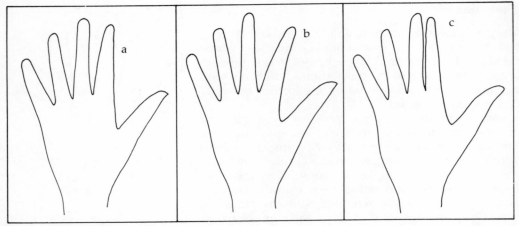

Figure 6

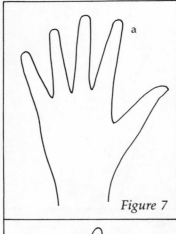

Figure 7

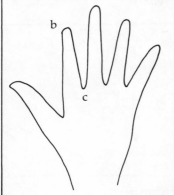

The index or Jupiter finger

This finger represents the conscious self, the ego, the individual's picture of herself and her standing in life. It gives information about her qualities of leadership, her socio-political and religious aware-ness and so often symbolizes the individual's ideas of politics, religion and the law.

When the finger is carried straight (Figure 6a) it denotes a good self-concept or a healthy image which is so important for the individual's self-assurance, self-confidence and standing in the world. If the finger leans outwards towards the thumb (Figure 6b) it reveals a goodly amount of ambition. Leaning the other way (Figure 6c) it indicates a person who shuns the limelight and who does not function well in a competitive environment. It has also been said that if the tip of this digit curves sharply towards the middle finger it is a sign of selfishness.

When the index is very long, that is, as long or even longer than the middle finger (Figure 7a), it reveals strong powers of command or of authority. On a good hand with many positive characteristics this would be one of the signs of a good leader. But, on an otherwise weak hand which highlights character flaws and moral weaknesses, it denotes the bully, the autocrat and the dictator. It has been said that both Hitler and Napoleon bore this formation. A marked lack of self-confidence is revealed by a very short index (Figure 7b), and if it is set much lower down into the palm than the rest, as illustrated by Figure 7c, it also suggests a strong inferiority complex.

A square tip to the index finger would show that the individual has a conventional and practical outlook not only about herself but also on all matters pertaining to religion, politics and the law. It would show strong leadership material with a tendency towards an ordered and structured environment. These people are often found in the legal profession or in the armed forces. Similar qualities would equally apply to a spatulate tip although this individual would have greater vision in matters concerning politics and religion but would probably be strongly impelled to either defend the downtrodden or take matters into her own hands when it comes to issues of law. A conic tip here reveals good self-confidence too and an easy-going, balanced attitude but probably changeable in her ideas concerning the important issues in life. A psychic-tipped index, which would be long, smooth and somewhere between rounded and pointed, shows a sensitive and impressionable viewpoint which is idealistic in the extreme. People with this type of index are often spiritually motivated and many of them are found amongst religious orders.

A long top phalanx to this finger would tell of an intellectual appreciation and understanding in all these matters and people with this formation would more than likely be directly interested or involved in politics, in religion and in all forms of the legal profession. Long middle phalanges here belong to financiers and company executives. Rounded or full-bottom phalanges on the index reveals the bon viveur, someone who enjoys food and the luxuries in life (Figure 8). Gastronomes, caterers and restaurateurs often possess this particular formation.

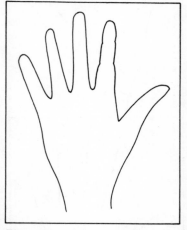

Figure 8

The middle or Saturn finger

The middle finger represents stability, responsibility, security, duty and sobriety. It can also symbolize contemplative study and research.

When this finger, together with the index, leans outwards it emphasizes ambitious drive (Figure 9a).

If, though, the middle and ring fingers both curve towards each other, as seen in Figure 9b, it highlights a conflict between a desire for independence, usually in order to pursue a career in the outside world, and a feeling of duty or responsibility to the domestic role. This is often seen on the hands of women who either decide to continue with their jobs despite the family (and consequently suffer terrible guilt pangs for it) or who give up the idea of a career altogether in order to devote themselves to their family and home (and as a result feel terribly frustrated and unfulfilled). Perhaps the solution for a woman who feels she has this problem might be to find a job which she can do from

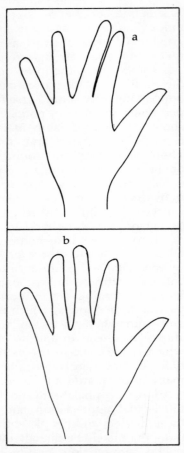

Figure 10

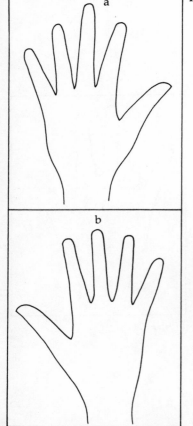

Figure 9

home, or share the domestic duties with her husband so that she can work at least on a part-time basis. In these ways she would be able to combine both needs in a happy compromise.

The middle finger is usually slightly longer than the index or ring finger but, if it is considerably longer (as illustrated in Figure 10a), it can suggest a lugubrious nature, someone who is pessimistic and a bit of a misery. When the finger is noticeably short (Figure 10b) it is a sign of unconventionality and those possessing this formation have an in-built dislike for rules and regulations and simply refuse to conform to or uphold traditional standards.

A square tip to the middle finger would denote a person with staunch conservative views. Conic would suggest a creative approach to one's environment, perhaps with a good eye for landscaping or property conversions. A spatulate tip might show adventurous ideas on land reform or the uses to which empty buildings could be put. It might also reveal an investigative and inquiring mind into all manner of research. With a psychic tip here it would show an idealistic attitude to all these matters and would probably heighten the individual's introspective powers.

A good student or excellent researcher is highlighted by an especially long top phalanx on this finger. It is also a sign of particular interest in occult or alternative subjects. An extra-long middle phalanx is associated with good management – of money, land, livestock, property or even of one's study or research. Thus it may be seen on the hands of good housekeepers, accountants, farmers or academics. A long bottom phalanx shows a special rapport with the land and a need for security and stability. Horticulturalists and farmers might show this formation but so too would someone interested in property, in bricks and mortar or real-estate. Some historians also have a long basal phalanx here. When short and rounded, however, it hints at the miser.

The ring or Apollo finger

The ring finger represents creativity and one's sense of personal fulfillment and satisfaction in life. It is the finger which rules appreciation of the arts, music and beauty.

A straight finger here which is also long and lean denotes excellent artistic skills and may be found amongst the finest painters or very talented actors and actresses. Generally, it is the sort of formation which highly creative people might possess or those who work constantly in the public eye.

When Apollo is as long or even longer than the middle finger it denotes the gambler (Figure 11a), a person who thrills at taking risks and chances. If it is very short (Figure 11b) it shows a lack of fundamental creative appreciation and as such might belong to a

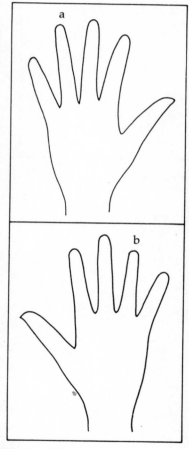

Figure 11

41

purely materialistic type of person who has very little time for cultural refinements.

The ideal ending to this finger would be the conic or psychic tip as these would bring out the best in terms of artistic and creative involvement. A square tip here might illustrate a practical application but perhaps at the same time might lack that necessary spark of inspired imagination. A spatulate tip in this position is perhaps most appropriate for the acting profession as it denotes dramatic talent or that spark of genius so necessary to the actress – although one should beware for this can also imply a tendency to mere exaggeration!

A long top phalanx emphasizes artistic appreciation whilst a long middle phalanx denotes a good eye for line and perspective. These are the practical artists, designers and creators. A well-rounded basal phalanx (Figure 12) is known as the 'collector's urge' and as such is found amongst connoisseurs and collectors alike, but only when the padding to the finger is high. If, however, there is no definite shape but the phalanx is simply podgy all over, it points to the out-and-out hoarder – that lady who just can't bring herself to throw anything out because it might come in useful again!

Figure 12

The little or Mercury finger

This finger represents communications and the media and thus symbolizes self-expression. It is also concerned with commerce, with science and with medicine.

Traditionally, it has been said that when a Mercury finger dramatically bends towards the ring finger it signifies dishonesty and duplicity (and especially so when accompanied by a markedly crooked index), although perhaps the better interpretation is that this is an inherited physical characteristic. But indeed, a long, straight finger of Mercury (Figure 13a) does reveal honesty, integrity and a strong adherence to the moral code. If the tip only should curve towards Apollo (Figure 13b) it highlights the person who is prepared to sacrifice her own dreams and desires for her loved ones or for the good of others. In short, it reveals an altruistic spirit. When the tip just barely,

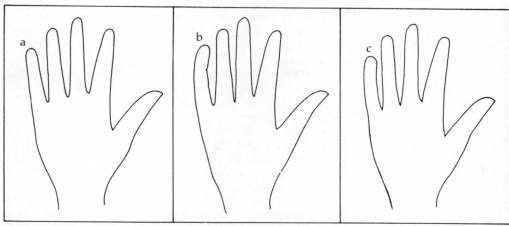

almost imperceptibly, curves (Figure 13c) it denotes a
person who is shrewd and sharp-eyed and who
possesses a goodly amount of insight and
perspicacity.

Figure 13

A very long finger of Mercury (Figure 14a) denotes
good literary talents. Those who write invariably
possess this formation, as do those who are witty,
natural orators, excellent conversationalists, and
superb after-dinner speakers, or those who are in the
media or who generally have the ability to express
themselves easily in either the spoken or written
word. Short fingers (Figure 14b) are quite the
opposite and these people show a marked inability to
verbalize their feelings and beliefs and, if the finger is

Figure 14

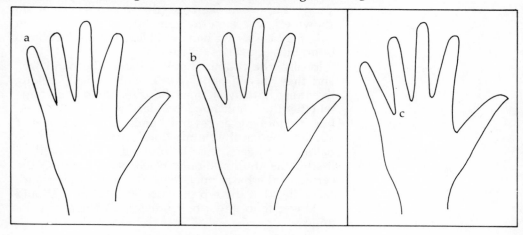

set very low into the palm in comparison to the rest, as shown in Figure 14c, it compounds this difficulty still further by adding a strong lack of self-confidence as well.

It is not usual to find a square or spatulate tip to this finger. It would normally occur only as part of a set and would be thus interpreted as a whole. The conic finger is more common here but if very psychic, verging on the pointed, communication skills might certainly be highlighted, with impressions and ideas being quickly and easily processed. A very fine and pointed tip, however, might also suggest a tendency to mendacity.

Always beware of the extremely long and pointed top phalanx on this finger (Figure 15) because it is a dead giveaway of the 'gift of the gab' and when you see it always ask yourself if you're being conned in any dealings you may be having with its owner. Some scientists or those in the medical profession often possess long middle phalanges on their Mercury fingers. A long basal phalanx here shows a need for the individual to express herself or to communicate to others whether through writing, broadcasting, in conversation or whatever means are at her disposal.

Figure 15

The thumb

The thumb is perhaps the most important of all the digits as it represents logic and strength of will. A strong thumb can overcome the weaknesses that are shown elsewhere on the hand but a weak thumb, on an otherwise strong hand, will lack the motivation to bring those qualities to fruition.

Ideally, the thumb should balance the hand well and they should both look as if they really belong together. Initially, it may be difficult to determine whether the whole hand is indeed well-proportioned but, by looking at several hands, it soon becomes apparent when the thumb does not complement the palm and fingers. Two helpful rules might be that, firstly, the thumb should reach at least up to the centre of the basal phalanx of the index finger and, secondly, that the top phalanx of the thumb should be longer than any other individual phalanx on the fingers.

If the thumb is proportionately too long or too large it suggests a forceful personality. When it appears heavy or bulbous the individual may be dominant and suffer from bouts of aggression. A short or overly thin thumb in comparison to the hand would make the individual a weak character, someone who is easily influenced and who lacks determination.

Figure 16

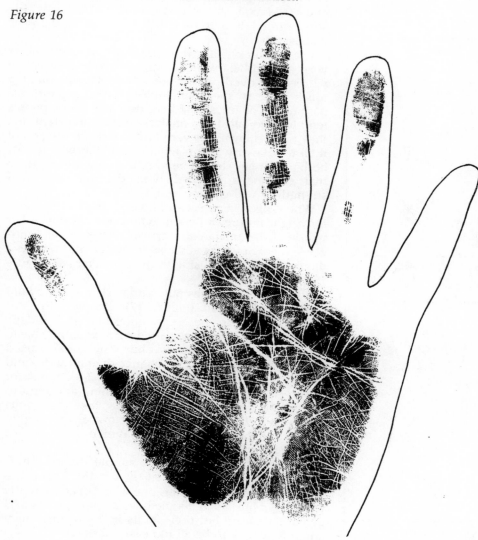

It is the top (or nail) phalanx which symbolizes will-power and this should be as long as the second one, if not just a little longer. The longer this section appears, the greater the determination and strength of will. People with a well-developed top phalanx here are often authoritative types who have the power of command. The broader it is, the more even and well-balanced the temperament but if it is thin and pointed it tells of a highly-strung and fretful disposition.

The second phalanx represents reason and logic. A very short phalanx here denotes instinctive action whereas an over-long section would suggest that too much time is spent on logically working out the parameters of any situation or decision. These people tend to rationalize and analyse to such an extent that they leave themselves very little energy at the end of it all to take any action whatsoever. For best results both phalanges should be roughly the same length so that reason is coupled with determination and strength of will is tempered by logic.

When this second section is very broad it denotes a forthright nature, a person who does not mince her words. If this phalanx is narrow, rather like an hour-glass, it is known as a 'waisted thumb' and reveals a diplomatic or tactful side to the character (see Figure 16).

A thumb which does not bend back at the top joint is classified as stiff (Figure 17). People with stiff thumbs tend to be very inflexible and indeed extremely stubborn. They are determined and able to concentrate for long periods but they are also fixed types and find it difficult to change their attitudes and ideas. Others find them somewhat 'closed' or 'reserved' for they are not forthcoming and tend to hide their feelings. Stiff thumbs take a serious approach to life and as such their owners are highly dependable with an unwavering sense of responsibility.

The opposite to this is the supple thumb which easily bends back at the joint (Figure 18). This is the mark of a flexible character, one who can adapt to the vagaries of life. Such people have an open, frank and generous nature but their faults lie in inconsistency and a tendency to be all too easily distracted.

Figure 17

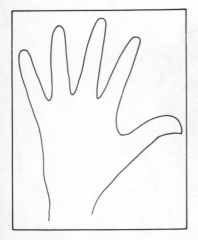

Figure 18

THE SPACING OF THE DIGITS

When the hand is placed comfortably at rest on a table or on a lap the fingers and thumb will fall into a natural pose. The pattern that is formed in this way by the digits in relation to each other is most important. This configuration can change under certain circumstances, for example, when an individual is going through a happy, relaxed time, the finger spacing may be quite different to when she is undergoing stress. Equally, there may be noticeable differences between the pattern formed by the right hand and that formed by the left. Such discrepancies may bring to light deep-seated conflicts or temporary changes of behaviour.

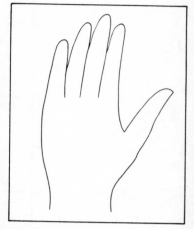

Figure 19

When all the fingers are held close together, as in Figure 19, it highlights a person who is quite content with her life and with the status quo. She may be reserved, or sometimes even repressed, but generally she is the dependent type who needs no challenges for stimulation.

If the thumb is held at an acute angle to the palm (Figure 20) it shows extreme introversion. This formation tells of terrific powers of self-control and, although the concentration and determination are sharpened, it suggests intensity and fixity of purpose. Sometimes this may be the sign of narrow-mindedness or limited tolerance. At other times it could be a valuable clue revealing that the individual is going through a stressful and anxious time, when she is mustering all her reserves and concentrating her energies in order to overcome her difficulties. This situation will be all the more evident if the tight formation occurs only on the dominant hand whilst the subjective thumb forms a wider angle.

Fingers which fall in an open formation, as seen in Figure 21, reveal a flexible and adaptable personality, someone who is cheerful, enthusiastic and optimistic in life. The hands of young children invariably form this pattern.

When the thumb also forms a wide angle to the palm it confirms the above but also adds an open and extroverted disposition (Figure 22). The wider the angle of opening, the less ability there is to concentrate at length and the easier the person

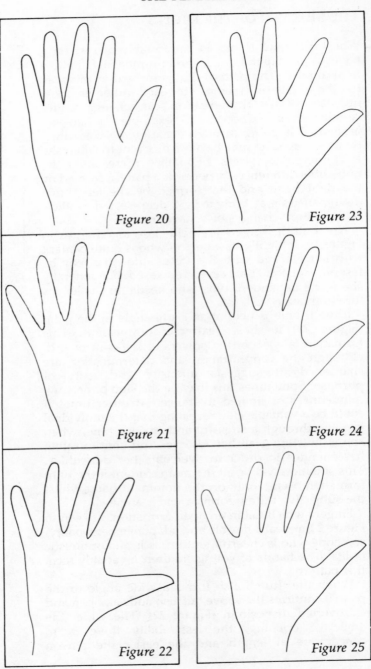

Figure 20

Figure 23

Figure 21

Figure 24

Figure 22

Figure 25

becomes distracted. When the thumb opens out to more than 90 degrees it highlights extravagance and a marked lack of inhibition. If the thumb on the dominant hand should spread wider than its counterpart on the subjective hand, it can suggest early restrictions (whether financial, physical or whatever) which, with maturity and independence, the individual has outgrown or overcome. If the reverse is true, where the subjective thumb is wider than the objective one, it suggests that either the adult life is tougher in some way than that of the individual's childhood, or, that the subject is undergoing temporary difficulties.

If the index finger forms a wide gap between itself and the others (Figure 23) it denotes independence of mind – an alert, questioning mentality which draws its own conclusions and is not swayed by other people's opinions or hearsay.

When the second and third fingers stand apart (Figure 24) it tells of someone who likes her own company, who needs time on her own to recharge her batteries. This formation on the dominant hand reveals that the individual prefers to work on her own. If it occurs only on the subjective hand it shows that as a child the person was a bit of a loner, possibly a bit shy, kept herself to herself and was perhaps a little antisocial. If these two fingers are held together they show a need for security, a gregarious nature which enjoys the company of others.

A wide space between the third and fourth fingers highlights the need for physical independence (Figure 25). This person would suffer if her liberty were in any way restricted. She has to feel free to come and go, even if she doesn't want to, but if her freedom were to be threatened or taken away then she would suffer mental torture. This also applies to any relationship she is involved in – if she feels trapped in any way she will feel very frustrated and will eventually rebel against it.

THE NAILS

The size and shape of the nail can give little insights into the character and disposition of the individual.

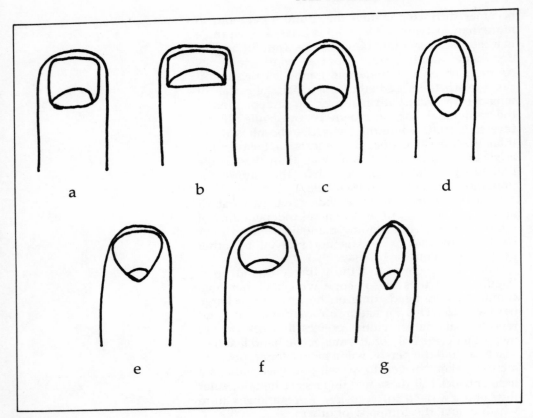

Figure 26

When analysing the nails consider only the pink or growing part because the top of it can be manicured and filed irrespective of its actual shape. Generally speaking, large nails depict broad-mindedness and tolerance whilst the short ones – when not bitten, of course – denote a critical nature.

Square nails (Figure 26a) suggest an even, placid temperament; they go with the square fingers and palm and thus reveal robustness and practicality. But, if a nail is much broader than it is high and so oblong in shape, it highlights an irascible temper (Figure 26b). More often than not when it occurs it is seen on the thumb and people possessing this type are fiery and quick to anger, erupting like a volcano. On the positive side, however, it must be admitted that they don't bear a grudge and an explosion at least clears the air so they don't end up sulking for days on end.

Large, filbert-shaped nails indicate an easy-going disposition, someone who is open and good-natured (Figure 26c). When upset, though, these women do have a tendency to sulk, and when they do sulk it can smoulder on and on and on.

Long narrow nails often reveal narrow-mindedness and a lack of versatility (Figure 26d).

The shell or triangular shape denotes sensitivity and people possessing this type of nail are often prone to stress (Figure 26e).

Rounded nails, particularly if they are short, highlight intuition but lack the practicality illustrated by the broader, squarer types (Figure 26f).

Long, thin, pointed nails have a cat-like quality about them and thus portray a scratchy and often bitchy disposition (Figure 26g).

THE MOUNTS

Finally, it is not possible to talk about the hand without a mention of the mounts. These are the fleshy pads which rise and fall like tiny hills all over the palm and it is the size and shape of each mount that reveals the vital energy that is represented according to its location on the palm. Taking into account the fact that the pad at the base of the thumb, which is called the mount of Venus, is usually higher and larger than all the others it is an interesting exercise to note which mount seems to be the dominant one, or which the most deficient, as this often provides a key to the individual's personality. Figure 27 shows the location of each mount on the hand.

The mount of Jupiter is found beneath the index finger and deals with the conscious self, the ego, the individual's perception of her standing in life and also with her ambitious drive. If the development appears too high in comparison to the others across the top of the palm then it hints at arrogance, at an over-weening self-confidence or self-importance which motivates the subject to strive for her own selfish ends. If this area seems flat and insignificant

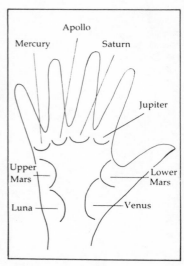

Figure 27

the individual lacks ambitious drive, is reticent about herself and her abilities and becomes prey to stronger, more dominant people. When the mount seems to be just right in relation to the rest it highlights a well-balanced self-image, with a positive attitude to life and a goodly amount of ambition – in fact a well-adjusted individual.

The mount of Saturn is placed beneath the second finger and represents stability, a sense of responsibility, contemplation and study. A large development here is not often found but when it is it denotes a melancholy, possibly depressive type who tends to be too introspective for her own good. So, in order for it to reveal a balanced sense of moral obligation and propriety, it is best if this area is somewhat underdeveloped.

The mount of Apollo deals with creativity, with the arts, with the individual's soul satisfaction and is situated beneath the ring finger. A well-proportioned mount here suggests a sunny, cheerful character, someone who is creatively gifted with a good eye for aesthetics and a love of beauty. If this area is proportionately too large or too high it can denote someone whose idea of beauty goes too far and becomes showy, ostentatious and brash. A deficiency here suggests a dearth of artistic appreciation or talent.

Beneath the little finger is found the mount of Mercury which represents communications, self-expression, science and business interests. When the area is well formed in comparison to the rest it shows that the individual is well endowed in these qualities. A good rich voice which may resonate or carry over distance, excellent powers of speech and of wit are all implied by this formation. In addition, these people may also possess business acumen or a strong medical or scientific bent. When deficient, it suggests a lack of self-confidence and an inability to express oneself. Too large a mount often points to the garrulous, over-talkative type.

Jupiter, Saturn, Apollo and Mercury form the band of mounts which are located directly below the fingers and beneath these still are found two more mounts, one at either side of the palm, which are known as the mounts of Mars. Upper Mars is situated towards the percussion edge, beneath the mount of Mercury, whilst Lower Mars is found at the opposite side, just above the base of the thumb.

Upper Mars deals with the individual's moral courage and resistance and when firm and well-developed it shows a person of integrity who sticks to her principles, who has the courage of her faith and convictions and who has the power of endurance in the face of difficulties. If this area is slim and deficient in appearance it suggests a moral coward.

Lower Mars actually portrays courage so that if the area looks well-formed it reveals a 'gutsy' person, someone who is active with plenty of energy and often sporty as well. A good development here tells of personal courage, the sort who would fight for her country and all the things she holds dear. She is the sort who loves a challenge and a dare, who needs the thrill of danger and so might enjoy more adventurous pastimes such as sky-diving, hang-gliding, moun-taineering or general deeds of daring-do. But, if this area is over large it suggests aggression, sometimes even leading to physical violence and this at all costs should be channelled into sports in order to diffuse the energy. A deficient or insignificant mount suggests a cowardly disposition.

Below this mount is located the ball of the thumb which is also known as the mount of Venus. This is an important area as it represents one's natural love of life. Invariably, this area is better developed than the rest of the hand, higher than all the other mounts and often taking up a good quarter of the palm itself. A normal development here reveals vitality, enthusiasm, zest for life, an extroverted personality who enjoys beauty, who is attractive because of her charisma and warmth and who is endowed with a healthy sex-drive. Moreover, people with this type of mount have plenty of physical resources and so often bounce back after ill health of any sort. But, if the mount is obviously too large in comparison to the rest and appears to dominate the palm, it shows someone who is prone to excesses, with a tendency to exaggeration, someone whose passions get the better of her and who is, in plain terms, over-sexed. A narrow, pale and weak looking mount reveals a bit of a 'cold fish', someone who is not out-going, lacks warmth of character and who is perhaps rather critical. Such people are not physically very strong and seem prone to constant nagging ill health.

On the percussion side, opposite to the mount of Venus and below upper Mars, is found the mount of Luna. This area represents the subconscious: imagination and intuition, instincts and impressions. A rounded development here would suggest a sensitive person, someone who is receptive to others and to the atmosphere around herself. People with a good mount of Luna have excellent powers of perception, with rich imaginations and a sympathetic understanding of all manner of flora and fauna. They readily empathize with other people and seem to have a special understanding of the rhythms and cycles of Nature. But an underdeveloped mount would tell of a lack of imagination and indicate someone who is perhaps not really in tune with her subconscious processes.

Chapter 3
THE GLAMOUR BUSINESS

Fashion is a critically important issue to most women, especially so because we seem to be bombarded from all sides by the media about what we should look like, how we should dress this season, what are the latest fashions, the 'dernier cri' of the designers. Hair styles, make-up colours, hemlines, legs, bottoms, bosoms – you name it – all come under scrutiny and are packaged neatly into the current 'look' of the day. Fashion, as we all know, is a multi-million pound industry with a fast turnover and a ready, eager following.

Of course, the dedicated follower of fashion is not unique to the twentieth century nor, for that matter, is it solely the preserve of the gentler sex. The briefest glance through the history books will reveal the changing trends – ruffs, bustles, crinolines, powdered periwigs – all had their time and place. Only in retrospect do we think how absurd some of these fashions are and yet, when it comes to it, we succumb to whatever fad is in vogue and don it religiously, like a uniform, lest we be thought of as fuddy-duddy or old-fashioned. How we cringe when we see photographs of ourselves ten, fifteen, twenty years ago: did we really wear our hair like that? Could we now stand, let alone walk, in shoes that high? We wouldn't even be seen dead in a skirt that length nowadays! Nevertheless we ought to hang on to our old clothes – these fashions are bound to come round again sooner or later!

But, when all is said and done, fashion serves many important functions, for apart from setting the scene historically, it also places people into recognizable peer groups, and often transcends social, political, economic or even religious beliefs. What fashion seems to do is to unify us somehow so that we feel we belong to a particular set and we can readily identify, feel comfortable or at home with other people who look and dress like we do and therefore who must think and behave like us, have the same hopes as us and dream the same dreams that we do.

Clothes are essential ingredients of the way we express ourselves, and the way we dress instantly reveals a lot about the individual for it is part and parcel of our body language. And of course it plays an enormous role when it comes to attracting others, especially of the opposite sex. Most of us at some time or other have made dreadful mistakes when buying or wearing certain types of clothes and it is only through experience that we learn which styles or colours emphasize our good points – and which our bad!

But there is a guide which perhaps could minimize those mistakes and help straight away to enhance our better qualities and that guide lies in the very shape of our hands. This is because the shape accurately mirrors not only one's personality but also the physical body, with its bone structure and its pattern of weight distribution. So, by understanding both the basic character and the body architecture as revealed by the hand, we can then interpret it into the sorts of clothes that express what we fundamentally are, that make us comfortable and that complement our personalities.

THE SQUARE HAND

Ladies with square-shaped hands are essentially practical, level-headed and down-to-earth. They don't go for frills or fancy ornamentation but, for them, it is the classical look, the functional, uncluttered, unfussy picture they prefer to present to the world.

Figure A

SQUARE HAND

Grace Crivellaro.

Figure B

They are hard-working people and so their clothes have to work hard for them too; they have to last a long time and they must be comfortable, practical garments which will keep their line and not require too much fiddly attention. Because they love gardening, walking and generally communing with Nature, ladies with square hands usually possess many sensible outdoor clothes. Teetering on four-inch stilettos certainly does not become them, for this belies their basic nature, but they must at all times look and feel comfortable and natural, with an honest-to-goodness aura about them. This type is often more conformist than the others and, especially as she gets older, may find that she dresses in a somewhat conservative style, tending to dress down rather than dress up. Oh, and by the way, throwing things away is quite painful for this type, especially if the garment in question is an old trusty favourite.

The colours that normally suit square-handed ladies are the natural, earthy and muted ones with lots of warm tones that reflect Nature. Fabrics, again, need to be hard-wearing and comfortable, such as woollens, tweeds, cottons – generally natural fibres are preferred to the man-made ones. Jewellery is never ostentatious. The pieces would, more than likely, be few but well-crafted, not necessarily expensive but certainly of good quality and sound value. When she wears perfume she would more than likely go for a heavy fragrance, a musk or perhaps a woody scent that is reminiscent of Nature, that evokes the countryside and autumnal wood-lands.

Figures A and B are a designer's interpretation of the types of clothes that would lend themselves to the character, physical structure and way of life described by the square hand.

THE CONIC HAND

Bring out the glamour for this type! Ladies with conic-shaped hands are imaginative and creative. They love all new ideas and thrive on variety and change. So, when it comes to clothes, they like to have their wardrobe full. These are the ladies who,

Figure C

CONIC HAND

Figure D

more than all the others, love to leaf through the fashion magazines and keep up with the latest styles, for they are extremely fashion conscious. Mixing, matching, playing with different styles and colours is all wonderful fun. And what's more they have a ready flair for combining and introducing the oddest elements, only to emerge looking like a million dollars.

Because these ladies are very feminine they can carry off frills and furbelows with great success. In fact, there's a vast range of clothes that will suit them – anything from the 'pretty feminine' right up to the 'vamp look' would still look good. They probably like to accumulate lots of accessories too, for in their hands a touch of this and a touch of that can transform any out-dated outfit into something bang up to the minute.

Not only will this type have a vast range of clothes but her colours will also be many and varied. Pastels will suit some of her moods but then so will bright, fresh, zingy and even jazzy colours too. And fabrics will be of all types for she also has the knack of very cleverly mixing natural and man-made materials, which all co-habit and rub shoulders happily inside her wardrobe. There will probably be a few shimmering dresses in there as well for she does like to sparkle now and then.

Jewellery, too, will be a mixture. There will be the inevitable delicate pieces which go with the frills, lots of costume jewellery to assist those 'transformation jobs' and big glittering rocks to add those sparkling splashes of glamour. Her taste for perfume will again change with her mood. A good stand-by will be a floral scent to go with her feminine clothes but, there again, the glamourous image will require a touch of spice!

The sort of designs which would suit the conic type are represented in Figures C and D.

THE SPATULATE HAND

There are two types of spatulate hands, one with the fullness at the base denoting physical power and the other, with the fullness at the top of the palm,

62

Figure E

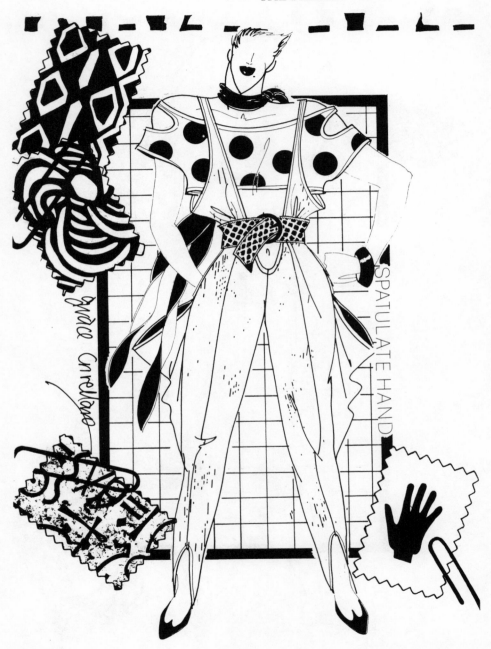

Figure F

64

denoting intellectual strength. Whether it be of a muscular or mental nature, both are characterized by energy, activity, vitality, and drive. Clothes, then, for the spatulate-handed ladies have to express the idea of movement; they must be comfortable, easy-to-wear and, in a lot of cases, sporty. Casuals, track-suits, trousers and sweat shirts are found in these ladies' wardrobes.

But then there's another side, too, – the adventurous one – for the spatulate hand is associated with explorers and discoverers. So perhaps there could also be a taste for fashion that conjures up far-away places – jungle prints, sarongs, silks from the far East. Continental designs, too, would probably attract this type particularly so if the emphasis is on the sporty line. Anything, in fact, with an overseas connotation would give them a lot of satisfaction. Of course, because of their adventurous and pioneering spirit, many of these ladies will travel extensively and one of their delights would include bringing back items of clothing from every corner of the earth to remind them of their journeys.

Ladies with a spatulate palm which is at its widest just below the fingers have good imaginative and inventive powers and, sometimes, their ideas can be well ahead of their time. This ability makes them excellent designers, especially so with their gift to create or anticipate fashion trends several seasons in advance. Although the actual designers amongst them are few, the others of this type are excellent at adapting old styles, innovating or simply trend-setting, for they are experimental and enjoy playing around with different styles. Some, as they get older, become eccentric and are known for their own particular style and yet others, because they live so much in their thoughts, may grow rather absent-minded and neglectful of the finer points of their dress.

For women with spatulate hands, fabrics that move are essential. Their clothes must not constrict or restrict and, above all, shoes must not pinch or be tight or uncomfortable in any way. Clothes or materials that give any hint of discomfort for this lady, that inhibit her activity or distract her from her objective by their awkwardness or unsuitability should, in her opinion, be burnt, torn to ribbons, thrown at the wall, jumped on or consigned, as speedily as possible, to the nearest rubbish dump!

Jewellery is either kept to a minimum, especially for the sporty ladies, where it would be quite discreet or, to satisfy the tastes of the more imaginative types, it would be ultra-modern. For some with this hand shape the most treasured pieces would most likely come from abroad, either given to them by admirers or brought back as souvenirs of their travels. The sort of perfume that would suit the sporty types would be fresh and clean-cut. The other type would prefer heady aromas evocative of Arabian Nights or fragrances that, redolent of incense, sherbet and spices, transport them to Turkish bazaars, to oriental temples, or to the mountains of Peru.

The designer's impressions capturing the personality and lifestyle of the spatulate type may be seen in Figures E and F.

THE PSYCHIC HAND

This lady has style. Whatever she wears she carries off as if it were *haute couture*. She is chic, sophisticated and elegant. She always seems to know just how far to go when putting her outfits together and achieves elegance through stunning simplicity. Quality is her keyword – quality rather than quantity every time. And detail, too, is of the utmost importance. An exquisite lace collar on a simple black dress, an embroidered panel, a piped lapel, a beaded glove: these are the highlights which she uses to focus the eye. Her clothes are never over-the-top, if anything, she underplays what she wears for she understands the power of subtlety. Each season she buys one or two items of the current vogue but she chooses them with great care and deliberation so that they will co-ordinate with the rest of her wardrobe and breathe new life into her favourite classics.

Psychic hands also reflect impressionability, romance: they are the dreamers, the poets, the idealists. Everything about them conjures up images of fragile pre-Raphaelite ladies swathed in flowing gowns. Indeed they do seem to live with their heads

PSYCHIC HAND

Figure G

Figure H

in the clouds and this shrouds them in a veil of mystery. Perhaps they can appear enigmatic at times and the way they dress reinforces the idea of mystique that surrounds them.

Colour, like detail, is used in a dramatic way, a splash of electric blue, perhaps, or a scarf to echo the tones of her skin – just enough to draw the eye. The fabric she chooses will echo the mood of romance: lace, silk, crêpe de Chine; it must hang, it must flow, it must drape. Whatever the material, it is always of excellent quality for it is the texture and the feel that make the impact. Quality, again, describes the jewellery preferred: simple, elegant, classical pieces, but well-wrought, of excellent craftsmanship and usually expensive. Her perfume always seems to linger, like whispers in the night, as if to testify that she has passed this way. Hers is a subtle, mysterious, dreamy fragrance which seems to have long, slender fingers that reach out and beckon you to follow.

Figures G and H are the designer's interpretation of the styles which reflect the type and personality of the psychic hand.

A question of weight

Hands, too, can tell us a great deal about those who are more likely to put on weight easily and those who are not and this is revealed primarily by the fleshiness of the palm and fingers. A person with a firm, lean hand where the bones are readily felt at a touch, is not likely to put on weight easily. But, someone whose hand is fleshy is going to have a much harder problem to keep her weight down, especially so if the hand is flabby, as this so often hints at a wee bit of indolence in the nature!

Notice, too, the basal phalanges of the fingers; if these are noticeably full, rounded and podgy then it is highly likely that this person will have a life-long struggle to keep herself in trim (Figure 28). If the fullness particularly relates to the basal phalanx of the index, this is a sure sign of someone who enjoys her food and who has a taste for the *dolce vita*. The distinction here between the one who prefers the art of cooking and the one who merely prefers eating, is that the former will have a full basal index on a firm hand, whilst the latter will have the fullness everywhere!

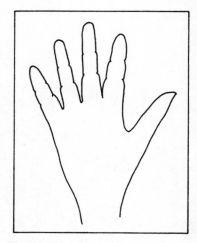

Figure 28

The question of weight is not only illustrated by the feel of the hand but it is also hinted at by the actual type and shape.

Square hands often reflect a fairly solid, well-built frame but, because this type is so busy and constantly on the go, excess weight can be controlled and kept down in this way. And, of course, the love of the open air means gardening and walking which is excellent exercise, keeping those extra inches at bay. Perhaps it is with maturity, though, that square-handed ladies are in danger of adding extra overall padding especially so if the hand is fleshy rather than firm.

Those with firm conic-shaped hands don't perhaps have quite so much trouble with their fingers as do the fleshier ones. There may, though, in both cases be a tendency towards the pear shape so exercise for this type would probably be a good thing.

Because the spatulate-handed ladies are known for their activity and their sporting interests it is not surprising to see so many of them in the gym or on the sports ground. Those who are physically active in this way can successfully keep themselves in good shape, although they do like food and they love experimenting with new tastes and all sorts of foreign dishes. But the others, whose activity is more of the intellectual kind, could do with following the example of their keener sisters, as some of that mental energy wouldn't go amiss if it were channelled, now and then, into a good physical workout.

The psychic hand is long and lean and, as such, suggests that its owner doesn't have a hard job to keep in trim. This hand tells of a tall slender frame and, because of her good sense of taste, this lady is more than likely going to stay that way. Although diet isn't so much the problem here, her urbane interests and way of life may mean that she doesn't get enough physical activity, and she would certainly benefit from some form of exercise. Swimming, in particular, would suit this type well.

Chapter 4
INSIDE OUT

In hand analysis it is the shape of the hand which, in describing the fundamental character, is laying down the skeleton of the personality. Just as a painter begins first with a sketch and then slowly, layer by layer, applies the paint and adds the detail, now the process of building up the profile can begin. Each section of the hand provides its 'layer of paint'; each line adds its minute characteristic, its strengths, its weaknesses, until the portrait is an unmistakable representation of the individual. When it comes to building such a 'portrait' of a woman through her hand, then, she may well find that she shares some of her characteristics in comon with others, some will be particular only to herself, but the combination and the way she deals with those characteristics is what makes *her* unique.

The skin markings, because they develop at the very early stages of foetal growth, begin the process from 'inside', as it were, and the information collected in this way lays down the first layer of the individual's disposition. The life line comes next and brings with it more information about the individual's temperament, about her physical state of being, about how she reacts to her world from the very core of her being. Slowly, then, in this way, from an entanglement of markings and lines, will the picture of a unique individual emerge in 3-D and in glorious technicolour.

SKIN MARKINGS

The surface of the hand, and for that matter the sole of the foot, is covered by a skin which contains the greatest number of sweat glands and nerve endings than on any other part of the body. A careful inspection of the hand will reveal that it is composed of tiny furrows which here and there form themselves into specific patterns. On the tips of the fingers, these patterns are recognized as fingerprints and, thanks to Sherlock Holmes, just about everyone knows that no two prints are ever alike – hence the need for such organizations like Interpol to lodge millions and millions of different dabs in their data banks which lead to successful criminal detection and prosecution!

In the Far East the uniqueness of each print has been recognized for many thousands of years and stories exist of the discovery of fragments of ancient pottery with the potter's thumbprint pressed into the base as his or her individual signature. But it wasn't until the end of the last century that the Western world suddenly heard of this phenomenon and Francis Galton subsequently pioneered the collection and classification of fingerprints as they are known today.

These skin patterns, however, occur not only on the tips of the fingers but all over the hand, particularly at the top of the palm beneath the fingers, on the mount of Venus at the base of the thumb and also at the opposite side, on the mount of Luna. The modern study of the patterns on the hand is now called dermatoglyphics. 'Derma' means skin and 'glyph' stands for a carving and together they beautifully describe those raised furrows or ridges which almost seem to have been carved out of the very skin upon which they lie.

The skin ridges on the hand develop in the early weeks of foetal growth and medical attention is now turning to dermatoglyphics and finding certain correlations between chromosomal abnormalities and particular skin patterns. Down's syndrome, or mongolism, is the best documented as yet but many other genetic disorders are being investigated at present. In simple layman's terms, the current supposition is that any genetic hiccup occurring during foetal development is somehow translated onto the actual skin formation resulting in abnormal patterns which, in turn, reflect the genetic abnormality. Some studies are being carried out which attempt to classify specific patterns on the hands of carriers of genetic defects and the hope is, of course, that the results could lead to useful genetic counselling in the future.

Although other aspects of the hands, including the lines, can and do change, the skin patterns remain the same throughout the individual's life. Even if the skin is cut or burnt the pattern will reappear in exactly the same formation after the injury has healed. They are our individual signatures – that part of us from which we can never escape and which sets us apart from every other person in the world.

There are several different types of fingerprints, three of which are the most salient, and the others are variations on the theme. The loop, the whorl and the arch are the most common and then come the tented arch, the composite and finally the peacock's eye. People do sometimes possess a full set of one particular pattern but this is by no means the norm. Usually, a mixture of prints is found and in these cases each type should be carefully noted and analysed individually. These patterns reveal fundamental dispositional information about the individual so it is always important to study them carefully.

Loops

Loops (Figure 29a) denote a flexible, adaptable approach in life. This is the most feminine of all the patterns and a lady who possesses a majority of this type has a creative and artistic flair. Variety is the spice of life for her. Being one step ahead, having lots of different things to do, surrounding herself with people in a free and easy atmosphere where news and views are readily exchanged is the sort of buzzing lifestyle or type of career in which she thrives. In any job, she is best working with other people, preferably as part of a team. But it should not be a humdrum affair because if she feels that she's in a rut then all her creative enthusiasm, her gaiety, her fresh inspiration, will all turn sour and she will start to vegetate. But generally, put her in any environment and she will simply get on with the job and make the best possible out of it.

When a loop is found on any individual finger amongst a mixture of other patterns, it should be interpreted as a flexible attitude to whatever is represented by that digit.

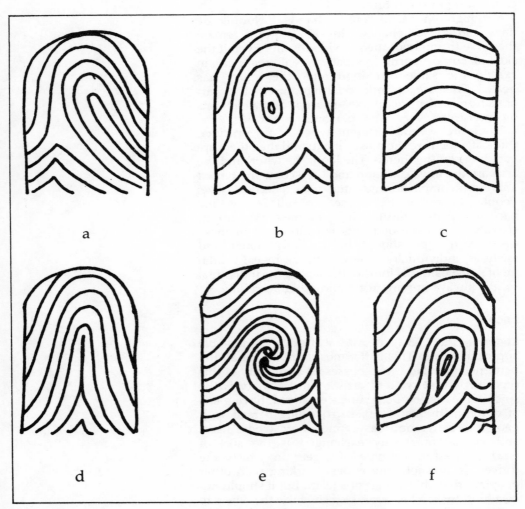

a   b   c

d   e   f

Figure 29

Whorls

The whorl (Figure 29b) is quite a different kettle of fish. This tells of an individualistic and somewhat fixed approach. Several whorls on a hand reveal a deep, quiet nature. Such a lady is fairly strong-minded, possibly the silent type, has set tastes and ideas and tends to resist change. To others she often appears slow, especially so in her response when her opinion is sought. The reason for this is because she needs time to mull over ideas and should never be rushed into a reply. To those who might get frustrated with her slow reactions, she should explain that she needs to go away and have a think first and when she has mustered her thoughts she will return with the answer. This is crucially important when any major decisions in life need to be made. She knows her likes and dislikes and because of her inflexibility or resistance to change she can seem stubborn and even pig-headed when her views and ideas are challenged. Give her time and if she agrees she will come round. At work, she is best doing her own thing in her own way. Trying to make her adapt or constantly looking over her shoulder will certainly not get the best out of her. Because she is a responsible type she will thrive in any job where she can be in charge or in control, so positions of authority really suit this type well.

A whorl is a strong pattern and wherever it occurs, on whatever digit, it denotes a fixed, possibly inflexible and certainly an individualistic approach to whatever sphere is represented. On the thumb, especially, it reveals a strong-minded individual who finds change of any sort very difficult indeed. Anyone who has this on her index should always try to find a job where she can be in charge, if not in total control, or at least where she is given scope to use her own initiative and perhaps where she can be left on her own to get on with it by herself. On the second finger, the whorl indicates fixed views on the basic ideology of life. A whorl on the ring finger tells of a keen creative eye. When it is present on the little finger, this pattern tells of someone who doesn't normally talk a lot – unless, that is, she starts on her favourite subject or is reminded of her pet dislikes.

Arches

The arch (Figure 29c) is a gentle pattern which denotes lots of common sense and a practical disposition. It tells of an earthy, sometimes materialistic, streak and a lady with several of these on her fingertips will always have plenty of concrete suggestions and advice to give. Airy-fairy, high-falutin intellectual theories are not her style at all – she relies on homespun truths and good old tried-and-trusted remedies which she knows have worked for generations of women before her. She is basically a solid, reliable and sensible type. Perhaps the one biggest problem that she is likely to possess is that she has difficulty in putting her innermost feelings into words and so she needs to find another means of expression, handicrafts, for instance, into which she can pour her soul.

It is rare to find a full set of arches and if so, they should be studied carefully as they may well be a sign of genetic abnormalities. But four or five prints may well be found on a normal hand which would certainly reveal all the qualities outlined above.

Tented arches

The tented arch (Figure 29d) looks basically like the ordinary arch but with a rigid line vertically through its centre. Normally, this pattern is found only on the indices and when present it describes someone who needs to be stimulated by challenges in life, or fired with enthusiasm for a project or a cause. Without this enthusiasm, life becomes very dull indeed.

Composites

Composite patterns (Figure 29e) are normally only found on the thumbs and indices. They look like two loops intertwined and give the impression of pulling in opposite directions. This is a most appropriate description because the pattern does actually denote a divided mind. An explanation of its significance invariably clarifies much confusion for the individual who possesses this pattern as it is indeed a complex sign. Basically, it reveals the ability to see both sides of an argument, to understand the other person's point of view. In any profession where judgements have to be made, such as a lawyer, a judge or a counsellor might be faced with, the capacity to weigh up the pros and cons of a given situation is not merely a useful quality but a necessity. So, under these circumstances the composites would certainly be an asset. But, when it comes to personal decision-making, this pattern can lead to much unnecessary complication. What can happen is that the subject tends to overthink, to work out the advantages and disadvantages so carefully that she ends up totally confused and bewildered and unable to take any action because each avenue of thought has as many positive outcomes as negative ones. The best advice here is for the individual to sleep on the problem and, on waking, to make the decision on gut reaction alone and thus, by trusting her intuition, she should not go too far wrong.

The peacock's eye

The peacock's eye (Figure 29f) looks like an elongated whorl inside a loop pattern and is more often than not found on the ring finger. When seen it has been traditionally described as a sign which reveals a sense of preservation or some sort of protection conferred upon its fortunate possessor. Palmists in the past have illustrated this with examples of people who have had lucky or even near miraculous escapes – crawling out alive from the wreckage of an aeroplane, pulled to safety from the top of a burning building seconds before it is engulfed by fire – and similar dramatic examples of people being saved from dire situations almost by the skin of their teeth.

PALMAR PATTERNS

Apart from the well-known patterns on the fingertips, those which occur on the rest of the hand, and known as palmar patterns, can also reveal much hidden potential and so should be examined as carefully as the fingerprints themselves.

Sometimes a loop may be seen lying on the palm just above the base of the thumb on the mount of

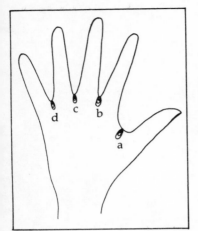

Figure 30

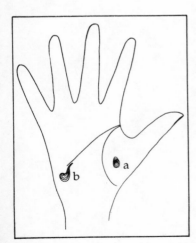

Figure 31

Lower Mars (Figure 30a) and in this position it suggests great physical courage. This pattern is not often found here.

Another unusual loop is that which is found between the index and the second finger (Figure 30b). Here it denotes leadership qualities or the power of authority and those with this marking invariably find themselves in executive or professional positions. In the Oriental tradition this pattern is known as the Loop of the Raj and is interpreted as denoting royal descent.

A loop between the second and third fingers (Figure 30c) is not so rare and when seen reveals a deep need for commitment or what may be termed as a vocational spirit, a desire to serve, a wish to be of use to the community or to give of oneself for the betterment of mankind.

When a loop exists between the ring and little finger (Figure 30d) it always denotes a witty and sometimes odd sense of humour. Certainly, this person can always see the funny side of life but what is even better is that she can laugh at herself and at her own mistakes. This makes her eminently human and means that she is better able than others to deal with the sort of lessons or harsh knocks that the school of life now and then throws at us.

There are a surprising amount of patterns which may exist on both the Venus and Luna mounts and these may take the form of loops, whorls or arches. Any of these patterns found on the mount of Venus, an example of which is shown in Figure 31a, usually suggests musical talents and an individual possessing one of these should be encouraged to develop those skills.

Patterns on the mount of Luna are most interesting for they have a variety of interpretations according to their position. Towards the centre of the mount, as illustrated in Figure 31b, suggests an attraction to water. A lady possessing this marking may find herself actually drawn to water, either enjoying boating or all kinds of water sports, or perhaps subconsciously choosing to live near a river or by the sea. And it is not unheard of that these people seem to take more baths and showers than others might! Whenever this lady feels low in spirits, needing a pick-me-up or has to make an important decision, a good piece of advice for her is to take a walk along a river bank or by the sea-shore as this will restore her flagging spirits and give her the necessary inspiration she requires.

A loop lying across the percussion (Figure 32a) reveals a wonderful rapport with all manner of animals and plants. Those with green fingers might possess such a marking and so too might someone with a natural understanding of animals of all kinds. The enjoyment of Nature, rambles or long walks in the countryside are a must for anyone with this pattern.

One that enters from the wrist at the base of the palm, (Figure 32b) is called the loop of inspiration. If a poet, a writer, an artist or anyone creative should possess this pattern then her work will surely stand out for it is marked with that touch of something extra. Great sensitivity for her work and the feeling that she plucks her ideas almost from thin air or that she is guided by some unquantifiable force might be the way she describes the influence of such inspiration.

Other patterns may occur on this mount but not enough research has yet been carried out to interpet their meaning satisfactorily. Often, however, these patterns suggest undeveloped latent talents, usually connected with creativity or with imagination and, because undeveloped, the subject may feel restless or frustrated, lacking in direction and spiritually unfulfilled.

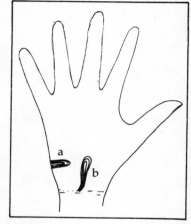

Figure 32

THE LIFE LINE

The life line represents the quality or tenor of the individual's life and not the longevity, as some people believe (Figure 33). It is within its very structure that much information about health and well-being can be gathered whilst the course itself will add greater insight into character and disposition. Important events such as emotional upheavals, moves or personal achievements, for example, are registered on this line in the form of cross-bars, branches, breaks, sister lines, etc. and, by

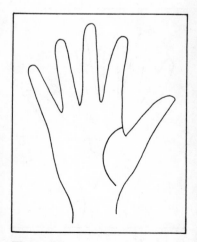

Figure 33

understanding the system of timing, any of these events can be pinpointed back in time. In the same way, the likelihood of such occurrences happening can be predicted for the future. A minute investigation of this line, then, will yield a rich crop of information which is central to the life of the individual.

Length

It is a common fallacy to believe that the length of the life line directly corresponds to the length of the life itself. Long lines have, in fact, been seen on the hands of people who sadly have passed away well before the termination of their own line. And conversely, short lines have been observed on the hands of nonagenarians who, according to the myth, should have left the mortal coil some fifty or sixty years previously. This belief is not only grossly erroneous, it can also be extremely dangerous and I have met several people who, having been told in their childhood that they possess short life lines, have suffered considerable anguish at the thought of premature death. One lady, I remember, had tried to put it out of her mind but, with the imminent approach of the supposed 'deadline', had found herself growing more and more anxious until she could no longer cope with her daily life. Another lady told me about a boyfriend of hers who also possessed a short life line and who again had been misinformed about it in his youth. Although an intelligent and rational man he had, nevertheless, accepted the fact that he was going to die young and so shied away from making long-term plans or committing himself totally to one woman. As a result he wasted much of his young life and it wasn't until he had passed his 'deadline' that he could start to lead a more fulfilling and rewarding life.

If the life line does appear short, as in Figure 34, it usually has a tiny hairline which connects it to either another section of life line or to the fate line, further towards the centre of the palm. This line, then, rather than illustrating a short life denotes a major change in the individual's way of life – a marriage perhaps which leads to a totally new environment, a move

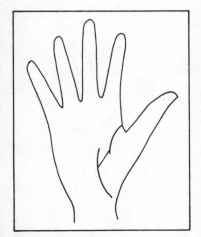

Figure 34

80

from one end of the country to another or maybe even emigration. Thus it isn't death that is shown in this way but instead a kind of rebirth, the chance to start a brand new life.

Sometimes if the short line is not seen on the major hand but only occurs on the subjective one, then it could indicate that the individual was born in a different country to the one in which she now resides. Alternatively, if she is a native of the country in which she lives, it could suggest that it was her parents who were the immigrants.

Course

The life line begins on the thumb side of the palm on average half-way between the base of the index finger and the beginning of the thumb. If it begins noticeably higher up towards the first finger, as in Figure 35a, the individual may be endowed with overweening self-confidence. A strong ambitious streak and powers of leadership are associated with this type of beginning.

Starting much lower down and closer to the base of the thumb, as illustrated in Figure 35b, suggests quite the opposite with a marked lack of self-confidence. Someone who is easily led, open to suggestion and who displays a sense of vulnerability or uncertainty

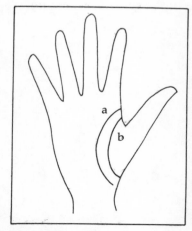

Figure 35

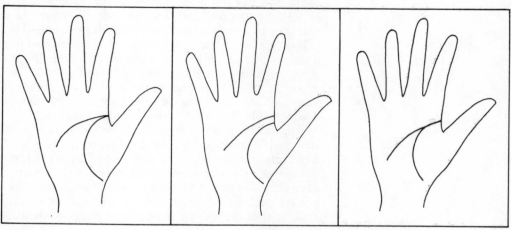

Figure 36   *Figure 37*   *Figure 38*

81

may be represented in this way.

The best indications are seen when this line begins either slightly detached from the head line or attached for only a short distance (Figure 36). These beginnings denote a well-balanced individual, someone who tempers caution with a sense of fun and adventure. An extremely wide gap between the two lines (Figure 37), reveals recklessness and impulsiveness. Someone with this marking would be quite a little daredevil, especially as a youngster and, if not mellowed through maturity, would adopt a 'live now pay later' attitude, taking risks and chances just to give life that little extra *frisson* of excitement.

If the two lines are intermeshed or attached for a considerable time, (Figure 38), the subject will be a late starter, possibly over-cautious, close to the family background and not developing her own sense of personal identity until comparatively late in life. This beginning is more often seen in the hands of ladies who were born several generations ago, who conventionally remained at home until they married. Under such circumstances, their more rebellious sisters, with the separated head and life lines, must have had a hard time indeed to curb their adventurous spirits and conform to the convention of the times. Nowadays, if a youngster does possess the long attached beginning she should be stimulated to think for herself and any signs of independence should be encouraged lest her development and maturity be overlong and more painful than need be.

The closer the line is situated to the thumb, so that it forms a small and narrow mount of Venus (Figure 39a), the colder and more distant the individual. Such a person might have a rather cynical or jaundiced view of life and she would lack a fundamental warmth which would make people somewhat wary of approaching her. Physical weakness may also be denoted in this way: the sickly child or the lady with a delicate constitution who finds it so difficult to resist disease or who can't easily recuperate after a bout of ill health. There is a marked lack of energy too and a certain pallor to the complexion, like that of a china doll, so that everything about them suggests delicacy and frailty.

But if the line sweeps generously around the ball of

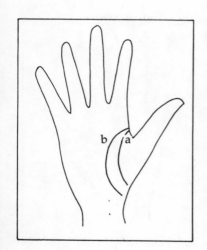

Figure 39

the thumb so that the mount of Venus is full and well-formed (Figure 39b), then the individual is outgoing with plenty of vitality and enthusiasm for living. She is endowed with what used to be called 'rude health', for her energy threshold is high and she is brimming with life. These are virile people, exuding natural human warmth and a certain *joie de vivre*; they love to love and equally need to be loved in return. They have a robust constitution and, after any bout of ill health, whether it be physical or psychological, they seem to have the ability to pick themselves up and carry on, much as if nothing had happened.

Structure

The line should appear strong and well-etched for best results and it should be of the same quality as all the other major lines. If it looks thin and shallow then it might suggest a lack of vigour or perhaps a nervous, highly-strung temperament. Very deeply grooved, though, could indicate too much intensity and single-mindedness.

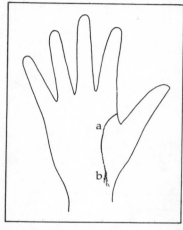

Figure 40

If the line appears at times strong and then thinner in places, as shown in Figure 40a, this would represent periods of constitutional strength and weakness and each period could be measured off and timed for the individual concerned.

Any fraying, tasselling or fuzziness in the line denotes dissipating energy. It is usually found towards the end of the line (Figure 40b), and suggests a loss of vital strength, often connected with the process of aging.

Islands represent a splitting of the life force which invariably means either a susceptibility to a particular disorder or indeed an actual period of ill health. When the islands are found right at the beginning of the line, just below the index finger, they can suggest a tendency to pulmonary/bronchial/respiratory problems (Figure 41a). If an island is seen lower down on the line below the middle finger it can be an indication of back or spinal trouble (Figure 41b). Further down still, towards the end of the line, an island may denote weakness or illness connected with old age (Figure 41c). Elsewhere on the line, the

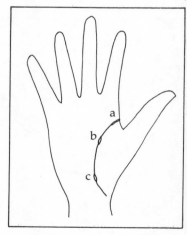

Figure 41

presence of an island can represent an accident or an injury, especially so if a strong bar also crosses the line at the same time.

Timing

Traditionally, of all the lines, this is the easiest one on which to apply the timing system and which also gives the best results. Because no two hands are exactly the same shape, however, minute adjustments of the system have to be made according to each individual. Once mastered, though, the gauge is simple and straightforward to use but, even so, perhaps the best thing to do is to double check by finding an important event which has been registered and then asking the subject for confirmation of the date. In this way greater accuracy can be achieved.

Figure 42 illustrates the method for working out the time system on the life line. This line is read from the top below the index finger and down towards the wrist. A vertical line, dropped from the inside edge of the index, usually strikes the life line at the point where it represents about 20 years of age. One millimetre roughly spans one year of life and so each millimetre can be marked off, forwards and backwards from the 20-year mark, thus establishing time on this line. It must always be borne in mind, though, that the scale is flexible and must be compressed or expanded according to whether the hand is unusually small or large. Any markings can then be read off against the scale and in this way events can be timed both for the past and also for the future.

Events

A bar which crosses the life line is known as a trauma line (Figure 43a). This indicates a time of crisis or emotional upheaval. These lines can be compared to the Richter scale which measures earth tremors – the bolder or longer the line, the greater the impact. A quick, short bar just lying across the life line and representing a temporary upset might be similar to registering, say, one or two on the Richter Scale. But a long, deep bar crossing several major lines and denoting a critical emotional upheaval could be

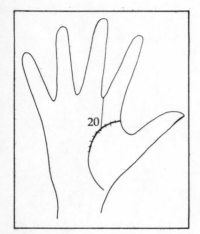

Figure 42

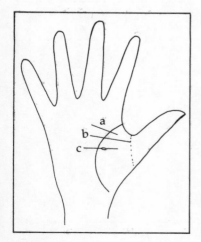

Figure 43

compared to at least six or seven.

If the bar line begins on or near the family ring, as in Figure 43b, the emotional upset is connected with relatives or loved ones. Opposition or interference from members of the family is sometimes represented in this way and is often the case if seen high up on the life line, around the late teens, when perhaps there is some family disagreement concerning the choice of girl- or boy-friends. The individual would register the emotional upset resulting from the inevitable rows and bad feelings as a strong bar line stretching from the thumb base and travelling right across the mount and across the main line itself.

If the trauma line crossing from the family ring should have an island in it (Figure 43c) then the worry may have something to do with the ill health of a member of the family.

When the trauma line stretches right across all the main lines – the life, fate, head and possibly even to the heart line (Figure 44a) – then the upset is extremely great, reaching the very core of the individual. For example, this might be found in the hand of a woman who suddenly discovers the infidelity of her partner, or perhaps in the hand of a wife on the point of divorce, or yet again representing the deeply sad loss of a loved one. This sort of line may denote different traumatic experiences for each individual but always with terrific repercussions and would reach pretty high on our emotional Richter scale.

Should the bar commence, not from the family ring but from an influence line (Figure 44b), the worry is centred around the person who is represented by that line.

If a short bar line occurs and directly below it an island develops in the life line, (Figure 45), it could be denoting an accident followed by a spell of ill health. Sometimes, a branch from this juncture shooting upwards in the direction of the second finger may represent consequent injury with possibly broken limbs or bones.

When these bars are very fine and there are lots of them all packed together across the line (Figure 46) they are not, in fact, trauma lines and do not represent specific events. Instead, they reveal a

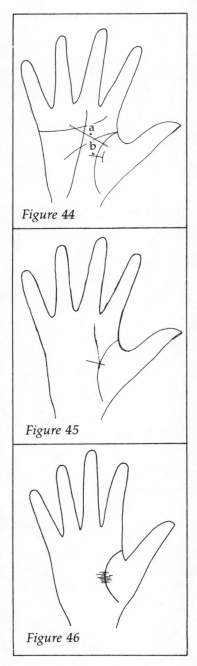

Figure 44

Figure 45

Figure 46

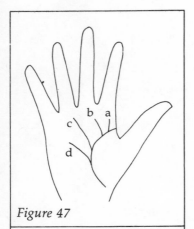

Figure 47

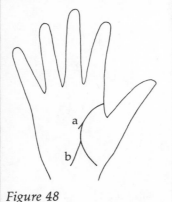

Figure 48

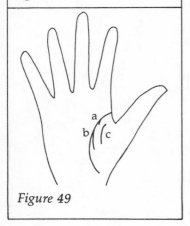

Figure 49

highly-strung nature, someone who has a tendency to worry unnecessarily and who is a fretful and anxious type of person.

Whereas bars crossing the life line are invariably negative signs, branches, which rise upwards in the direction of the fingers, are positive signs of achievements. A branch rising towards the index finger (Figure 47a) often denotes academic success – good school results, examination passes, Degree or professional qualifications are often represented in this way. Towards the middle finger (Figure 47b), a branch suggests successful property negotiations; buying the house of one's dreams, perhaps, or maybe going into the real estate business. Leading towards the ring finger (Figure 47c), denotes achievements connected with creative or artistic subjects or possibly just a sense of personal fulfilment. When a branch is seen reaching towards the little finger (Figure 47d) then financial deals, literary or scientific successes, or even commerical achievements have been attained.

A branch which shoots downwards, however, is called a travel line. This represents not only journeys but movement of any kind which is important to the subject. Changes of address, for example, as in Figure 48a, are seen in this way, whilst a major journey, perhaps overseas, is illustrated by a longer branch sometimes stretching as far as the mount of Luna, (Figure 48b).

Now and again little branches may be seen springing from the inside of the life line and these represent influences or relationships. The presence of a tiny branch (Figure 49a), may correspond to the birth of a baby whilst a longer one (Figure 49b) could denote a partner or spouse. Another way a marriage partner may be represented is by a parallel line running inside the main line itself (Figure 49c). The point at which these branches commence will denote the year in which the baby is likely to be born or the relationship to begin.

If there is a line running parallel almost all along the length of the main life line, (Figure 50), it is known as a sister line or line of Mars and has either of two interpretations. It could represent an influence that is so strong in the subject's life that it almost forms part of her. A partner who is more of a soul-mate than a husband, for instance, might be registered in this way. Alternatively, it can suggest a form of physical strengthening, especially so if the main line itself is chained or weakened in some way. In this case, the sister line acts as a back-up of some kind, a secondary line of defence or hidden reserves which the subject can call upon when needed.

Breaks in the line denote changes – sometimes occurring quite suddenly. A clean break, (Figure 51a), which is extremely rare to find, may represent a sudden bout of ill health or an accident. Should a square formation be seen covering over the break (Figure 51b), then traditionally this means that circumstances will somehow cushion the individual in such a way that she is protected against the full gravity of the situation.

If the break is, in fact, an overlap, as in Figure 51c, it indicates a change in the way of life usually because of a move or a change of circumstances which takes the individual into a new situation or environment.

What is interesting with all these breaks is to analyse the new section of line and to see where it is situated. If it is as strong as before then the new life continues as strongly as ever. But if the new line is weaker, and shot through with islands or crossing bars, then the ensuing life may not be of the same quality as before. The position of the new section also gives important information on the state of the new life. If the line recommences behind the old one, that is, closer to the thumb (Figure 52a), it suggests that the change results in a more constricted or restrained type of life than before. But when the new line restarts further out towards the centre of the palm, (Figure 52b) the promise is of a much wider, fuller and more expansive way of life than before.

Each of these events can be easily measured against the time gauge and a clear idea of the possible ups and downs in life can be established. Once we are able to define the likely occurrence of particular events in our lives, we are no longer powerless, no longer vulnerable, no longer at the mercy of our circumstances; for then we can have the power to act, to control our own destinies. There is great merit in the saying 'forewarned is forearmed' and being able

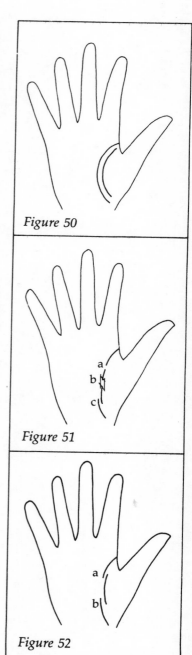

Figure 50

Figure 51

Figure 52

to detect the possibility of an impending emotional crisis, for instance, means that we can spot the danger signals well in advance, and so deflect the problems, skirt around them or, if they seem absolutely unavoidable, at least brace ourselves in preparation for the onslaught. The important thing is not to let ourselves be caught unawares for this is when the body blow knocks us off our feet.

Equally, if we notice that a positive event is marked in the near future, for example a branch towards the index mount implying academic successes, we would be able to confront any impending examinations with greater confidence, and perhaps perform that much better too, instead of suffering paroxysms of nervous anxiety. A word of caution, though, lest the presence of any feature should lead to complacency – there is no inevitability in the hand and an indication can just as easily disappear again if the subject does not actively work towards its fruition.

So it is by studying our hands, and in particular our life lines, and by learning to recognize the signs and the changes, the ups and the downs, that we can then always be one step ahead – no longer the victims but now the mistresses of our own fate.

Chapter 5

WORKING WOMEN

One of the most rewarding aspects of hand analysis is that of career guidance. All of us, no matter what our backgrounds or status, are richly endowed with gifts, talents or abilities which are specific to each individual and these talents, whether they be latent or overt, are clearly represented in our hands. What we choose to do with these talents, whether to use them or allow them to remain dormant, is of crucial importance to our personal development and to the whole course of our lives.

We cannot all become gardeners or painters or doctors for we may not all possess the essential qualities required for such occupations. And then some of us who might have the right aptitude for a particular profession may not get the opportunities, or the necessary training, in which to develop the requisite skills. A young woman, for example, whose hands show all the signs of a good mathematical brain would therefore, let's say, have the ability to make an excellent architect. The fact that her parents, perhaps, are not well off and that she needs to work in order to supplement the family income means that she has to stop her studies prematurely and thus never realize her full potential in this respect. Nevertheless, given her mathematical talents, she might be able to choose a more immediate occupation which would still require her flair for numeracy as a trainee accounts clerk, for instance, or in banking, and in time she would be able to develop her talents by working her way up along these lines.

It must be constantly remembered that we are not predestined for only one particular course in life. The individual can be infinitely flexible and, taking the above example still further, it can be seen that the same young lady's mathematical brain could, under different circumstances, take her into engineering, astro-physics, teaching, medicine, astronomy, she could become a cashier, a computer programmer, a croupier or successfully enter into a variety of other professions.

Those people who are able to use their innate talents in a career are lucky indeed but, bearing in mind the present difficulties in the employment situation, many women just have to accept whatever job they can get, frustrating as it might seem. But even here hand analysis has an important role to play because, by unravelling all the natural abilities of the individual, a woman can be guided into channelling her talents, if not into her main career, then at least into hobbies and pastimes. In this way she will at least find personal satisfaction and the sense of purpose and fulfilment which she might otherwise never achieve in an unrewarding occupation.

Advice concerning careers can be invaluable at almost any time in a woman's life. A parent, understanding her children's hands, will be more aware of the potential of those youngsters and so will be better able to encourage or provide the right environment for them to develop their abilities. Advice on the correct choice of academic subjects would also be easier to give by knowing the sort of signs to look for on the hand. When it comes to actually choosing a career, understanding the indications on one's own hands can certainly help to narrow the field of possibilities. Later on, when a woman considers going back to work after her children have grown up and left home, hand analysis can offer much encouragement and an objective assessment of her position. Equally, when someone finds herself at a crossroads or lacking direction, a quick look at her hand will reveal the problem and offer possible solutions. And right through the whole course of one's working life the hand will show the likelihood of changes, of achievements, of problems and successes which will then allow the individual plenty of time and scope to prepare for such eventualities.

When looking for clues on occupational or career matters the shape of the hand should be considered first. This was dealt with in Chapter 2. However, the two main areas of investigation are centred around the head and fate lines. Additional information is scattered all over the hand in the form of anomalous markings or special features which highlight vocational direction or inherent talents.

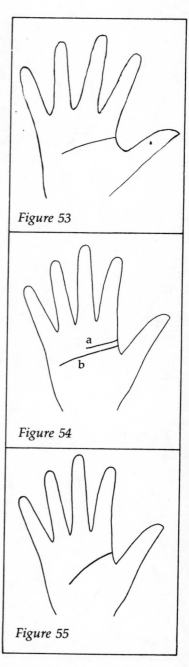

Figure 53

Figure 54

Figure 55

THE HEAD LINE

The head line is, I believe, the most important line for it represents the individual's mental processes and intellectual capacity (Figure 53). It tells us how the individual thinks, whether she has problems, anxieties, is a clear thinker, cool and rational, imaginative or neurotic. By examining this line minutely it can reveal intellectual peaks and troughs, it can predict times of possible success and achievement as well as periods of confusion and self-doubt. Moreover, the strength of the head line marks out those who are leaders and those who are followers.

Direction

When the line lies straight across the palm (Figure 53) it represents a practical, pragmatic, logical or analytical mind which can also sometimes be introspective. A lady with a good academic mind who possesses this line might show a leaning towards science, mathematics, technology, engineering or any of the 'hard core' subjects. If she is practically orientated she might choose business studies or secretarial work or otherwise any job which requires a practical mentality.

If the line is long and straight, as depicted in Figure 54a, it indicates a theoretical and analytical mind. But, when the line is short, it highlights interests which are more concrete or mundane so that a lady with a short straight line would tend to see her world in tangible materialistic terms (Figure 54b).

The opposite of the straight line is the bowed line (Figure 55). This one represents the sort of mind which enjoys diversification. Someone with a bowed head line will be much more interested in the arts and humanities for it tells of a creative and imaginative mentality. There is a wide spectrum for this lady to choose from. She may enjoy languages and anything to do with communications, writing, working in the media perhaps, or generally dealing with people. Literature, history and any of the 'softer' subjects would appeal. If she has great talent she would make a fine painter, designer or illustrator. Alternatively, a career as a dancer, hairdresser, florist, dressmaker, flamboyant cook or any other profession requiring creative flair would suit this type.

A line which begins straight and then half-way across starts to dip downwards reveals a good balance of a scientific and creative mentality (Figure 56). A person with this type of line might be uncertain which direction to choose. If she goes for the purely scientific she could well feel that her creative impulse is stifled and if she chooses an out-and-out artistic course she may find her logical and analytical powers frustrated. What she should try to do, then, is to find a job or career which will allow her plenty of scope to use the two in harmony; where she can balance the pragmatic side with the creative one. In the academic world the social sciences seem to bridge this gap and any subject which encompasses the concept of man within his environment or any other structure, such as geography, architecture or even the law might be suitable. A career as a bilingual secretary, for instance, is another good example which combines the two.

If the head line curves in a long sweep right down into the Luna mount it reveals an extraordinary imagination (Figure 57). An artist or a writer of fiction would do well to possess such a line as this. But the richness of the imagination may often come dear to the people with this marking for it can sometimes run out of control, leaving the individual moody and melancholy. At its worst this line can describe the

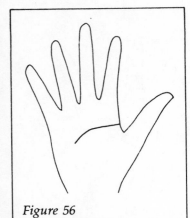

Figure 56

Figure 57

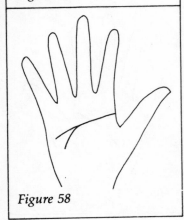

Figure 58

neurotic or even the manic depressive but, at its best, it can produce the finest artistic creations imaginable. Ladies with this line should learn to harness their imaginative powers and, rather than allow themselves to be carried away, they should channel them into tangible creation, thus producing something positive and worthwhile.

A head line which splits into two directly beneath the ring finger is known as the writer's fork (Figure 58). Not all writers have this marking nor, indeed, do all who have it become writers. It does, though, reveal good powers of creativity and as such may be seen on the hands of artists and designers. For someone who does want to make her living as a writer and who possesses this line the actual formation of the fork should be studied carefully. If both the prongs project down into Luna she should concentrate solely on fiction. When both tend to travel in a straightish course across the palm the mind will run more towards factual, documentary or biographical writing. Journalists sometimes have this type of line but, if the two parts are widely separated so that one lies across the palm and the other shoots downwards, then this lady would be more successful at writing faction or dramatic literature.

Figure 59

A fork which is seen on the head line developing below the little finger is invariably the sign of a good business woman, someone who may like to run the whole show for herself (Figure 59). This is often a most encouraging sign for a woman who is thinking of taking up a career in mid-life and who feels she has talents or skills she could develop or exploit in this way. So, a forked head line below the little finger signifies business acumen and should spur all those who have this marking to think up ways and means of setting up a business of their own for this would certainly give them tremendous satisfaction and fulfilment.

The Simian line is fairly rare on a normal hand and is a line which comprises both the heart and head lines into one straight groove right across the palm (Figure 60). It does, nevertheless, exist in a small percentage of hands and, whenever seen, the line reveals intensity. A lady with a Simian line, therefore, would have a convergent mentality and a

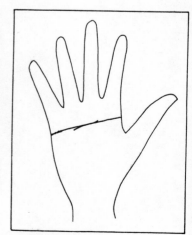

Figure 60

strong ability to concentrate. She would find it extremely difficult, however, to diversify or to think about several things at once – whatever she is working on at one particular moment in time receives her full and undivided attention. When the task is finished she will go on to the next and give that her full concentration in turn. So, the sort of job that would suit this lady is one in which she can quietly work in logical sequences, one thing at a time, and certainly not be expected to deal with many diverse issues or cope with lots of different problems all at the same time.

Discrepancies between right and left

When there are distinct differences between the head lines on the right and left hands then hand analysis becomes really fascinating. Any discrepancy denotes a difference of attitude between the public and domestic side of an individual and also between the youngster and the mature adult. So each line has to be interpreted separately, according to whether it is found on the objective or subjective hand and the information should then be applied accordingly.

For example, consider the case of a right-handed lady whose head line on the left hand is straight whilst that on her right is gently bowed. This shows that as a child she would have appeared to be more scientifically or practically minded and would therefore have shown greater flair in these subjects than in the artistic ones. She might have gone so far as to choose and enjoy a career in, say, physics. As she matured, however, she would have discovered that a strong creative side to her mentality was developing and that she needed more diversification in her job than she had originally imagined possible. If her career was sufficiently flexible to allow her greater creative expansion then all would be well and good and in her case she would be able to side-step into an applied area of her subject. But, if she originally chose a rather fixed and inflexible occupation, then she would grow increasingly frustrated by a lack of stimulation and would be faced with a decision either to put up with an unfulfilling career (and perhaps find satisfaction in spare-time activities) or resign from her position and try to find something more suitable to her new intellectual needs.

When analysing the head lines, then, it is essential to work out and understand both of them in conjunction with each other. In recognizing the growth patterns that are revealed between the two it would be possible not to fall into any traps by making premature decisions which the individual may one day regret or outgrow.

The beginning of the line

For a confident, well-balanced approach to work, and indeed to life, the head line should be either just separated from the life line or only attached for a very short distance (Figure 61a). When the two lines are widely separated it tells of someone who is prepared to take risks and chances (Figure 61b). She will be independent, extremely adventurous and quite a daredevil, especially as a youngster, and if not taught the meaning of caution may even be foolhardy and reckless. At work such an indomitable spirit would enjoy life on a knife-edge so anything with a sense of adventure would be ideal for this type – stunt work, horse-racing, steeplejacking, aerobatics – if it's dangerous then she's bound to love it.

When the two lines remain attached for a considerable distance, stretching beneath the entire base of the index finger, then the individual will be extra cautious and almost painfully timid (Figure 62). This shows a clingy, dependent type who might be described as a late developer. Once the two lines separate, however, she will find her own independence and begin to stand on her own two feet.

Structure

The very structure of the head line itself is vitally important, illustrating the way an individual thinks and thus becomes most relevant when considering career prospects. The line should appear equal in strength to the rest of the lines because if it is weaker and the heart line is stronger, let's say, it intimates that the emotions take precedence. If the head line is the strongest groove in the palm it would suggest

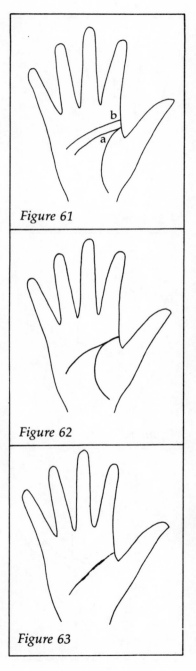

Figure 61

Figure 62

Figure 63

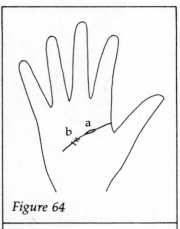

Figure 64

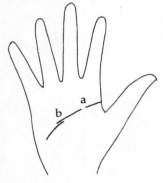

Figure 65

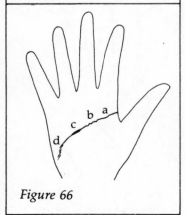

Figure 66

that the intellectual powers are the most dominant, driving force of the individual.

A strong well-etched line shows clarity of thought, the ability to make sound decisions and a good strong mentality with the power of leadership. But if the line is faint, fuzzy, blurred or chained it denotes woolly-mindedness, a weak mentality that is easily influenced or led and one which has difficulty in decision-making (Figure 63).

An island occurring in the line indicates a time of worry and anxiety which lasts for the duration that the island exists (Figure 64a). Sometimes this worry may also be coupled with feelings of self-doubt. Although the anxieties inferred by the island could very well be centred around any area of the individual's life, the fact that they are represented here would, of course, suggest that they do interfere with the normal, everyday thinking and therefore would also have their repercussions on the smooth routine of the individual's working life.

Bars which cut across the line also denote interference and set-backs and these could represent, for example, conflict with a colleague at work, thwarted progress in one's career or opposition to one's ambitious goals (Figure 64b). A careful study of the head line after such times of interference will tell whether or not the conflict has left any long-lasting detrimental effects. If the line regains its former strength then the effects have been negligible but, if there are any signs of weaknesses or breaks, then the events have certainly left their damaging marks.

Should the line show a sudden and clean break it is a very rare sign indeed and may, in certain cases, denote an injury to the head (Figure 65a).

Quite different is the indication where the line does break but is overlapped by a brand new section of head line (Figure 65b). Here it would tell of a radical change in the individual's thinking, but it would not be a sudden volte-face because the overlapping lines denote a gradual process of change. This would show that the individual slowly begins to question her philosophy of life; her views, opinions and beliefs come under scrutiny and she reconsiders her own ideas, her aims and objectives in life. Such a time of mental reorientation is normally triggered off by an important event, the breakdown of a marriage, perhaps, or maybe the discovery of new political or religious awareness, and the indications of these catalysts would be registered elsewhere in the hand.

Any tiny dip in the line forecasts a period of depression or flagging spirits (Figure 66a). If the line appears to zig-zag, no matter how minutely, it denotes intellectual peaks and troughs, times when the thought process is constructive and clear followed by flat, uninspiring periods when the mind is at a low ebb (Figure 66b). Should a section look broad and fluffy, as in Figure 66c, it denotes a lack of concentration and personal uncertainty but, once the line resumes its normal structure, the strength of the thinking process is once more restored.

Fraying which, if it occurs, is usually seen towards the end of the line, suggests memory loss and is often one of the indications of senility (Figure 66d).

If any of these features should appear on the line, the individual has plenty of time to anticipate the events that are indicated and can prepare herself to skirt around the issues, try to prevent them from happening altogether or, if they are absolutely unavoidable, to at least arm herself against the onslaught!

Branches

Sometimes, tiny branches may be seen shooting downwards off the main line. These should not be confused with either the writer's or business forks for these branches, as illustrated in Figure 67a, are very small indeed. When they appear they invariably indicate a time of depression or deep emotional upheaval and if the head line is examined carefully, other evidence such as an island, a bar or a dip in the line may very often accompany this feature.

Branches which shoot upwards towards the fingers are quite another matter. These are always positive signs of intellectual achievement. When a branch rises towards the index mount it suggests scholastic or academic success (Figure 67b). If the branch were to shoot up in the direction of the Saturn mount, as seen in Figure 67c, it would have either of two interpretations. Firstly, it might indicate a realization

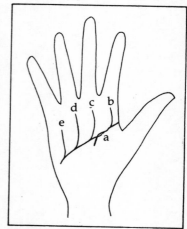

Figure 67

of one's aims or ambitions at work or, alternatively, it may be seen in connection with successful dealings to do with property. A branch going towards the ring finger denotes a sense of creative achievement (Figure 67d). And if the branch should shoot up towards the little finger it could well signify business, financial or even scientific success depending on the subject's career (Figure 67e).

Timing the head line

It is possible to time all the events shown on the head line by applying a time gauge similar to that used on the life line. But it must always be remembered, however, that precise accuracy to the very day or even month cannot be achieved in hand analysis and that is one of the few limitations of this discipline. Nevertheless, with practice and experience it is possible to predict the likelihood of events within a year, or even a half-year, and to be able to refine it thus far must still be of great value when one considers that events don't usually happen overnight but are a part of a sequence or process and that planning for the future is invariably a long-term project. Remember, too, that the gauge is flexible, as it needs to be compressed in a small hand and expanded for a large one. Because of this it is always wisest to ask the individual for confirmation of at least one date and then work backwards or forwards from there. Finally, when dealing with the head line it must be constantly borne in mind that its length does not in any way denote longevity.

Timing of any line is best applied to a print of the hand where accurate measurements can be taken. Figure 68 illustrates how to divide up the head line on a print. First, draw a vertical line down from the inside edge of the index finger – the point at which it meets the head line is roughly twenty years. Another vertical line dropped from the centre of the base of the middle finger cuts the head line at around thirty-five. Working from these dates, each year, which is represented by about one millimetre, can then be marked off along the whole length of the line.

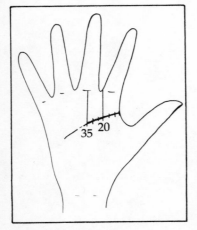

Figure 68

THE FATE LINE

The fate line is a most wonderfully useful line to analyse in connection with one's career for it not only gives clues as to the way an individual applies herself to her work but also registers movement and changes within her occupation and way of life.

Beginnings

The fate line travels vertically from the base of the palm upwards towards the fingers. It can have any of several starting points but its commencement is important to note.

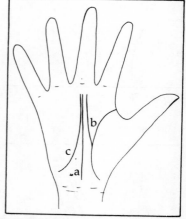

Figure 69

Traditionally the fate line is described as beginning at the wrist right in the centre of the palm and travelling in a straight line to end on the mount of Saturn (Figure 69a). This sort of line would illustrate a person whose life is, in a sense, pre-ordained or already mapped out for her. She would follow a conventional life, where each turn is pre-planned, with a somewhat fatalistic attitude. This line, although it does still exist, is rather rare in these days of social mobility when a woman has greater freedom of choice and when the employment needs are so changeable.

If the line springs out from the body of the life line or even from inside it, it shows early committments and responsibilities to the family (Figure 69b). A woman with this sort of line might have had to sacrifice her own independence in order to care for a sick mother, for example, and it isn't until the fate line separates that she can then break the ties and begin life in her own right. Because of the sense of duty that was imposed on her in her early years, this configuration always denotes a person who has an old head on young shoulders. Moreover, success for her, in whatever sphere she chooses, comes only after much hard work.

When the line begins on the mount of Luna, as depicted in Figure 69c, it tells of someone who needs to work with other people and preferably, if at all possible, in the limelight.

Sometimes the line may not occur until a little higher up in the palm (Figure 70a). When this is seen

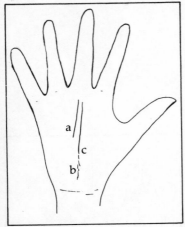

Figure 70

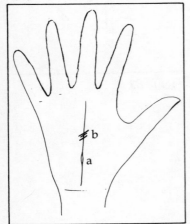

Figure 71

on a lady's hand it suggests that she doesn't quite get to grips with the reality of her life until the line actually develops. That is to say, she may not consciously feel in control of her own destiny, of herself within her environment. When, in fact, the line does eventually begin, it marks the development of a sense of responsibility and she will then feel that her life and career are beginning to take shape.

If, at its beginning, the line is fragmented it denotes a lack of direction (Figure 70b). This might well describe a youngster who goes from one job to another trying to find what she really wants to do in life. It might also portray someone who is unemployed and is trying, with a growing sense of hopelessness, to find a job. This sort of line, then, shows an uncertain, vacillating lack of purpose and it is only when the line strengthens into one solid groove that she finds direction and stability in life (Figure 70c).

Negative markings

If, continuing up the line, an island should appear it indicates a time of dissatisfaction (Figure 71a). This might be due to worries about work, possibly financial problems but a general frustration or disillusionment with the way the career or life is progressing.

Bars that cut across the line denote interferences or opposition (Figure 71b). This may come from a set of circumstances, an associate or colleague at work which either block, check or set back the individual's hopes and aims. If the line regains its strength after these indications then the negative influence was short lived but if, however, the line weakens in any way then it would seem that the events leave a lasting and detrimental impression on the life of that individual.

Event markings

The slightest change of course seen in this line directly represents a change within the career and/or way of life (Figure 72a). This is the sort of indication that is seen when perhaps a lady is promoted or takes on new responsibilities. Check the structure of the line before and after the deflection in order to ascertain whether the change has been favourable or detrimental.

If the line should come to an end but another section overlaps it and continues upwards, it tells of a complete change of job or career (Figure 72b). The size of the gap seems to be relative to the type of change so that, if it is a small gap between the overlap, it might suggest a simple and straight-forward change of job. But, if the new section begins a good distance away, it could denote a major change of career which might even entail a move from one part of the country to another.

A completely clean break with no overlapping lines denotes the sudden end of one career or way of life and the beginning of another (Figure 72c). This might occur when a lady is suddenly made redundant, for instance, and the beginning of the new line suggests the picking up of the threads or the start of a new job. Whereas the fate line with the overlapping sections denotes that the individual herself is making the change and planning the move, here the sudden break shows that the individual has no control over the situation and she is either at the mercy of the prevailing circumstances or of the machinations of others.

Branches stemming off the fate line are usually favourable indeed. One that travels towards the index finger might suggest success in the academic world, in politics, in religion or anything to do with the legal system (Figure 73a). As the classical ending of this line is on the Saturn mount, a branch to this area would not normally be found. Towards the ring finger, as seen in Figure 73b, suggests creative fulfilment or satisfaction in one's career but care should be taken not to confuse this with the Apollo line itself which sometimes has its roots in the fate line. Rising towards the little finger might imply financial rewards or any achievement within the realms of science, business or communications (Figure 73c).

On some hands a multiple of fate lines may be seen and these always suggest great activity (Figure 74). A lady who perhaps has two part-time jobs, takes care of the accounts for her husband's business in the

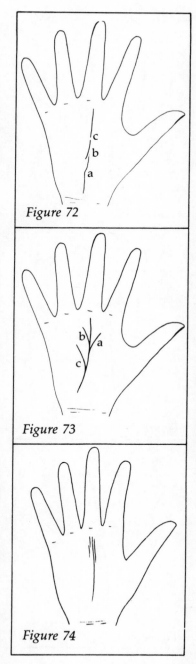

Figure 72

Figure 73

Figure 74

101

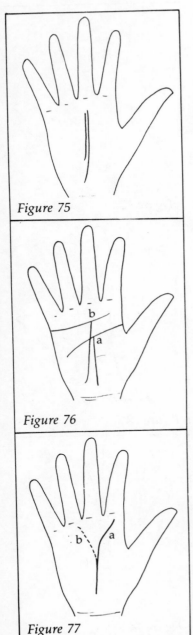

Figure 75

Figure 76

Figure 77

evenings and still has time to look after a house and children might possess this type of configuration. Alternatively, a lady whose job requires her to wear many hats in the course of a normal working day might also show these markings. A plurality of fate lines, then, usually denotes a 'Jill of all trades' and one of the consequent problems of so many disparate activities is that, in dispersing her energies and attention, she may never attain full-blown success in any.

Two parallel lines, though, have several interpretations (Figure 75). One might be that it illustrates a woman with two major interests in life – a career woman, let's say, who is also a town councillor in her spare time. Another interpretation might suggest a business partnership and a third could feasibly imply a husband or lover who is considered not simply as a spouse but more as a partner in life.

It must be remembered that, similar to those on the head line, any of the markings seen on the fate line are only indications that the events are likely to occur. So, when considering future predictions, once armed with the knowledge of these possible eventualities one can then begin to take evasive action, in the case of the negative markings, or be alerted to the opportunities suggested by the positive ones.

Termination of the line

The classical and most usual ending to this line is on the Saturn mount just below the middle finger. If the line should end on the head line, without a new section taking over from it, it suggests that a serious misjudgement has been made which cut short what might have been a promising career (Figure 76a). Ending on the heart line implies an emotional blunder such as a public scandal, for instance, which then loses the individual her credibility and blights her career (Figure 76b).

If the fate line crosses both the head and heart lines and then, instead of ending on the Saturn mount, turns and ends on the index mount, this suggests a career in the public eye (Figure 77a). People who are in the media may have this feature or who receive daily recognition and approval from the public. And if the line should swing over towards the ring finger it implies a career given over to the arts which brings much creative fulfilment and satisfaction (Figure 77b).

Retirement

It is interesting to examine that part of the fate line which exists above the heart line as this indicates one's retirement and old age. Depending on the size of the hand, the point at which the fate line crosses the heart line is around the late fifties, add another few millimetres and there roughly is the section which represents the retirement age. Very often a hand will show breaks or a change of direction in the fate line at this point which logically can be interpreted as coming to the end of one's working life and sometimes even a move to, with luck and forethought, one's ideal retirement home.

Some people plan carefully and meticulously for this period in their lives and look forward to it as a time in which they can do all the things that busy careers and responsibilities prevented them from doing. Others consciously avoid the very thought because a job for them means a sense of purpose, of camaraderie and identity. So they come ill-prepared to their retirement and stare across years of emptiness and loneliness.

Analysing this part of the fate line, then, will give many clues, well in advance, of the quality of those years. Whatever indications exist, an individual would be able to lay down some long-term plans, perhaps start new projects for her old age, take out medical insurances, consider where she would like to live or prepare for whatever will then most enrich her life.

If no visible signs of breaks or detours exist then it is quite possible that no changes will take place for that individual. Perhaps she will be asked to stay on at her job indefinitely or maybe her way of life will simply continue with no apparent differences. If, at this point, the line doubles or even triples it indicates a retirement full of activity when she will cram in all the exciting things she has always wanted to do (Figure 78a). Branches at this level, going towards the

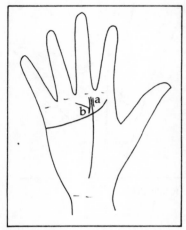

Figure 78

index or ring finger, as shown in Figure 78b, suggest an expansion or development of the self – in the former instance mixing with more people possibly, or an awakening of interest in politics or religion; and in the latter case, a development of the individual's creative or artistic potential.

If islands or bars are seen, however, as in Figure 79, they would herald less pleasant times ahead and this is where forward planning would come to the rescue. Islands here might denote financial restrictions or disappointments whilst bars highlight interference and opposition. Should these markings be seen, then the individual could well consider putting aside a nest-egg perhaps, or taking out an insurance policy which would mature at the appropriate time, thus ensuring independence and cushioning herself for the future. When this type of premeditated action is taken it is not unusual to find that the negative markings will disappear with time. Further indications regarding this part of one's life may be found on the Apollo line which is described on the following page.

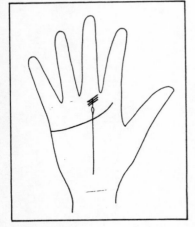

Figure 79

Timing the fate line

As with the head line, the time gauge is best applied to a print. The line is read from the base of the hand upwards so, following the illustration laid out in Figure 80, measure the fate line from the top rascette ('bracelet' line) at the wrist right up to the bottom joint line which connects the middle finger to the palm. Halve the line and this is about the thirty-five year mark. Applying the gauge to this line is a little more complicated than on the head line because not only does it have to be modified according to the size of the hand, but it must also be expanded below the thirty-five year mark and compressed above it.

So firstly fit in 0 to 35 years either by halving and quartering that section of line until each year is marked out or, alternatively, by taking just over a millimetre for each year. Then, above thirty-five, compress the gauge by marking off yearly intervals of just under one millimetre each. Once the fifty year mark is reached, it is possible to compress the gauge a little further still until the whole line has been thus

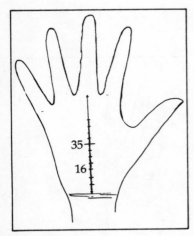

Figure 80

104

divided up. Remember, it is always advisable to corroborate the timing system by confirming the date of an event with the individual concerned and then any necessary adjustment of the scale may be carried out from there.

THE SUN LINE

The Sun line, otherwise known as the Apollo line, represents one's sense of creative satisfaction and fulfillment. This line may be difficult to find on some hands as it can begin almost anywhere and on a few hands it may not even exist at all. It can be found, however, by tracing it back from its ending position just below the ring finger. The Sun line can be used in conjunction with the fate line as they seem to work together and support each other. Any breaks or weaknesses seen on the fate line may be backed up by the strength of the Sun line, thus showing a cushioning effect of the circumstances surrounding the events at that time.

A line which begins low down on the palm near the wrist is a rare marking and would suggest fame or public approbation at a very young age (Figure 81a). A child protégée, young actress or pop singer might have this feature in her hand.

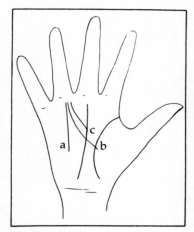

Figure 81

If the line should begin from inside the life line it usually suggests that family influence has helped that person to attain success (Figure 81b). But, when it springs out from the life line itself it indicates that any achievements or successes have been won through the individual's own efforts and hard work. When the Sun line is seen as a branch off the fate line it suggests that creative fulfilment has occurred as a result of the individual's career – work satisfaction might be described in this way (Figure 81c). People in the public eye or in the media might possess a Sun line which begins on the mount of Luna. This feature invariably shows public recognition (Figure 82a). Higher up, from the mount of Mars, as in Figure 82b, this line tells of success which comes a little later on in life and usually only after much hard work on the part of the individual.

In many hands the Sun line only occurs above the

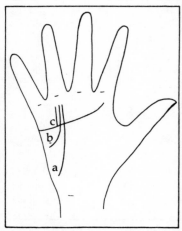

Figure 82

heart line and in this position augurs a happy and contented old age, one that is filled with much love and affection (Figure 82c). This is indeed a splendid marking to possess especially when considering one's retirement years. Three parallel lines above the heart line, as depicted in Figure 83, have a classical interpretation which says that such an individual should not worry about money for she will always have enough to get by. This does not mean to say that she will necessarily enjoy riches beyond her wildest dreams but merely that, whenever she needs money, it somehow comes to her, even at the eleventh hour.

Figure 83

SPECIAL EFFECTS

Apart from the shape and the lines, there are other particular markings or features all over the hand which give specific clues to innate talents or to vocational direction. I call these the 'special effects' as they add that little bit extra to any analysis. Such markings do not imply that an individual is necessarily predisposed to a particular career or style of life, they merely represent inherent gifts which could be developed should the subject choose to do so. Very often, as these talents are part of the individual's birth right, to ignore them or prevent their full expression can often be detrimental to that person. Those who feel frustrated, unfulfilled or who lack direction may suddenly find the way again or become stimulated and invigorated by discovering that they posses a particular innate talent and that, in developing it, they often rediscover themselves and open out a whole new exciting life.

The medical stigmata

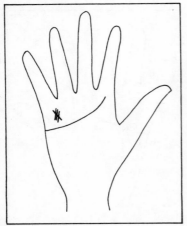

Figure 84

This feature consists of three vertical lines, often crossed by a horizontal one, which lies on that part of the palm immediately below the ring and little fingers (Figure 84). When present this marking indicates a natural gift for healing. Those who have felt the urge to become doctors, nurses or vets may indeed posses the medical stigmata and, although they may not have had the opportunity to train for any of these

106

professions, they could still use this wonderful talent in everyday life. They might become interested in spiritual healing, for example, or in herbalism or alternative medicine. But a woman with this marking need not actually practise medicine in order to express this talent for she may well be in social work or in counselling, for example, and the innate disposition to which this points would make her just that little bit more sympathetic or empathetic in her job. For those in the medical profession the medical stigmata indicates that intangible quality that gives a person that special 'bedside manner'.

Most interestingly, I have discovered a link which sometimes occurs between the medical stigmata and backaches. It seems that in many cases people who do not use this skill to their full potential often complain of back pain of one form or another. The only way I can describe it is that in healing one uses an energy or force of some kind and the individual, in not using that talent, is not channelling the energy outwards but trapping it and the ensuing 'blockage' causes the pain or discomfort to the lumbar region. This, however, is as yet undocumented elsewhere and is a result of my own findings; more research requires to be done here in order to establish the connection.

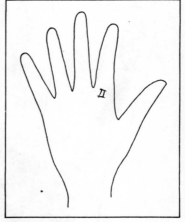

Figure 85

The teacher's square

This formation, which is illustrated in Figure 85, lies on the mount below the index finger and is composed of four tiny lines which form themselves into a square. When it is seen it denotes the ability to impart information or, in other words, a natural flair for teaching. Those who possess this marking make sensitive and understanding teachers, whether in academic institutions or simply to their own children.

The creative bow

A hand which noticeably bows outwards at the percussion edge indicates strong creative powers (Figure 86). A lady with this type of hand should try to make her career in any of the artistic or creative fields, especially so if this structure is accompanied by a curved head line.

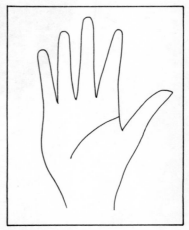

Figure 86

Figure 87

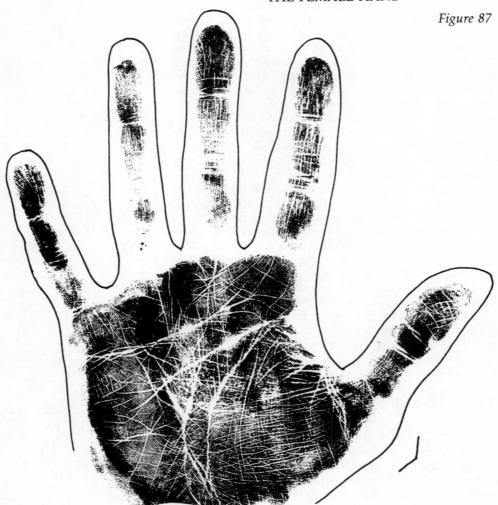

The angle of manual dexterity

This formation is seen at the base of the thumb where it meets the palm (Figure 87). If the angularity here is very pronounced it signifies excellent manual dexterity so anyone possessing this formation is basically good with her hands. Manual work, handicrafts of all sorts, do-it-yourself jobs, any occupation that requires skilled hands, nimble fingers or intricate handiwork would suit this type well.

The angle of rhythm and timing

The angle of rhythm and timing is another angular formation this time occurring further down, as illustrated in Figure 88, where the palm meets the wrist. As its name implies it reveals a sense of timing and that is why so many musicians possess this feature. So very often when seen, it does highlight musical talents – if not a practising musician then at least someone who has a good ear for music.

In the few instances where this formation exists but where the subject insists that she is tone deaf and only ever dares to sing in the bath, it would still reveal a sense of timing. In these cases it might represent a strict sense for punctuality, or maybe she is excellent at the sort of sports where timing is of the essence or possibly, like a comedienne, she has the knack of delivering a punch line just at the right moment for maximum effectiveness.

Flora and fauna

A skin pattern in the shape of a long loop entering the palm from the percussion edge and lying across the mount of Luna reveals a natural understanding and rapport with plants and animals alike (Figure 89). Those who possess this marking are gentle nature lovers and would do well in any such allied occupation.

Vocational work

A loop which occurs on the palm between the second and third fingers, as illustrated in Figure 90, invariably denotes a vocational urge to do good works for the community. Anyone with this marking, then, should consider social work, becoming a member of the council, joining community schemes, VSO, any occupation requiring vocational dedication or, alternatively, any voluntary work of benefit to the community at large.

Communications

A long little finger, especially if it is pointed, reveals a good speaker, orator or literate wit (Figure 91). A lady with this feature would excel in the media or in an

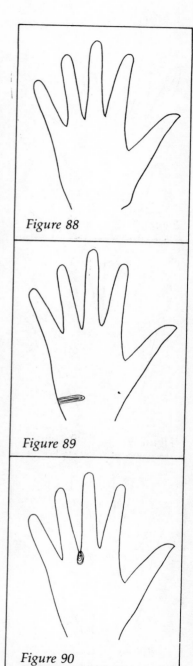

Figure 88

Figure 89

Figure 90

109

Figure 91

Figure 92

Figure 93

occupation where she needs to constantly deal with and communicate with others. Advertising or PR work immediately spring to mind, as does any form of selling – particularly with the pointed fingertip which shows that she would be able to charm the birds off the trees!

Catering

When the bottom phalanx of the index finger is noticeably full and rounded – sometimes even podgy – it reveals someone who enjoys food and all manner of culinary delights (Figure 92). These people may find that they gravitate towards the food industry: becoming cooks, going into the catering business, joining courses on *haute cuisine*, owning restaurants or, if not, then simply enjoying the art of cooking for its own sake.

Gardening

A full and rounded, or sometimes even long, basal phalanx on the middle finger often highlights a flair for gardening and someone who is reputed for her 'green fingers' might well possess this formation (Figure 93).

Collectors

When the bottom phalanx of the ring finger is full and round it is known as the collector's urge (Figure 94). People in the antique business often possess this formation or indeed anyone who has a penchant for collecting beautiful things. There is, however, a subtle difference to be aware of here because it is only when the padding is full but well-shaped that it indicates the true collector. When, in fact, it is full and round but not in a high dome shape it simply denotes a hoarder!

The bow of intuition

As shown in Figure 95, the bow of intuition is a semi-circular line which is found on the percussion side of the palm. When present it symbolizes an extremely sensitive and highly intuitive nature and as such represents an invaluable gift for anyone whose career

110

or profession involves the care and understanding of others. Anyone in the medical profession, counsellors, problem-solvers, clairvoyants and such like would certainly benefit from this very special talent.

BOSSES AND WORKERS

As well as career guidance, hand analysis can also be used to facilitate relationships between the employer and the employee. Quite understandably in this situation it may not be at all practically possible to grab your employer's hand in order to study it at length and just as tricky to attempt to analyse in depth the hand of an employee – both actions could prove awkward in the extreme, let alone embarrassing! Under these circumstances, however, a quick glance is often enough to give a good idea of another person's character and disposition, and would give sufficient information to reveal compatibility or at least to give some strong hints on how best to relate to that individual.

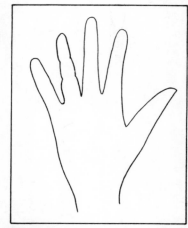

Figure 94

None of the pointers which are given here are intended for any Machiavellian or manipulative purposes. Rather, the guidelines for both employers and employees are suggested in order to make all those who have to work together, staff and management alike, that little bit more understanding and tolerant of each other. The days of 'us and them' must surely be well and truly over now in these times of economic depression when the aim of the whole work-force should be to pull together, for the good of the company, institution, corporation, or whatever, in order to secure a stable and profitable future for all concerned.

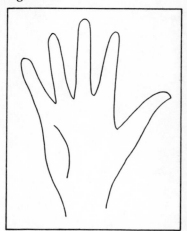

Figure 95

Employers

At some point or other we all become employers – if only when we get the gas man in to check over a faulty cooker, or we take our car in to the local mechanic to get the brakes checked. In some situations our interactions with these people may only need to be brief and relatively inexpensive, but at other times our involvement might be a lengthy one and may incur thousands of pounds' worth of work. Calling in a builder to add an extension to the house might be one such case in point. Negotiations with the notorious second-hand car dealer might be another.

In such circumstances where we can contact several companies and talk to different representatives, builders, salesmen or the like, we have the opportunity to compare their hands just at a quick glance. Here, the elements to be on the lookout for are the type of hand shapes, the length of the fingers, the size and shape of the thumb and any other features which instantly stand out.

Firstly, establish the requirements of the job and then try to fit those parameters to the appropriately shaped hand. For instance, if the job requires a lot of constant, solid, hard work then go for a square hand but if it is an intricately artistic job then try to find someone with a long, psychic hand. A person with short fingers will give inspirational work although it may be somewhat hit-and-miss at times, but if careful precision is required then go for long fingers every time. Always watch out for a very long and pointed little finger as this can mark out the charmer, or con artist. Finally, there is sometimes a particularly squat, bulbous thumb, in the case of a man, or a thin, very pointed one, in the case of a woman, which, when accompanied by crooked fingers, can indicate a somewhat unscrupulous, mendacious type. So, although it is not recommended to make hasty generalized judgements, it would be wise to check on these people's reputation and credibility before entering into any important negotiations or business dealings with them.

For a boss of a company a quick look at her employees' hands could prove invaluable especially at the initial interview stage. Again, establish the specifications of the job and then match them to the right sort of hand shape. For instance, square hand shapes belong to solid, hard workers who like to work in a systemized fashion – but remember that they like routine and if your company is on flexi-time or split shifts then this employee might feel quite unsettled in her work. If you need someone with an eye for detail, who will work carefully and meticulously then a lady with a long palm and long fingers would suit the bill.

If at the first hand-shake the hand feels firm then this would indicate an energetic worker, but a flabby hand makes for a lazy, indolent employee. Look at the thumbs for signs of strength or weakness – if strong this lady has the potential to become a good leader, but if the top joint is very pronounced she is likely to be stubborn and pig-headed. The question here is: in any critical issue would she meet you half way or would she simply dig in her heels and refuse to compromise? Alternatively, would this feature suggest guts and determination in carrying out a job? It would require a deeper analysis to answer these questions but the cursory glance at least brings attention to this area.

A very long index finger, especially if it stands apart when the hand is at rest, denotes a strong ambitious streak and you should ask yourself whether this position is merely a temporary stepping stone for her or whether, in a few years' time, this candidate will be after your own job! If the thumb is stiff in appearance and held tightly close to the palm it could well suggest an introspective person, one who may not get on easily with her fellow workers. But if the area on the palm just below the little finger is large and puffy to look at it pinpoints a warm, sociable individual, albeit loquacious at times. A thumb which is 'waisted', or looks like an hourglass, denotes a most discreet and tactful disposition. If the work involved is rather sensitive or if it requires someone with a strong sense of diplomacy then a person who possesses this thumb would certainly fit the bill.

The type of mentality, and whether the candidate will be loyal, reliable or conscientious in her work really does require deeper analysis. However, it can be seen that a cursory glance at the hand in this way does at least provide many clues and alerts the attention to all sorts of characteristics, both good and bad, which might be of crucial significance to a prospective employer.

Employees

Employees can just as well apply the above categories to their bosses and also to their fellow workers in order to understand them better, noting the hand shapes (for basic compatibility of character), finger lengths, and qualities revealed by the thumbs. For instance, a good clue to look out for is a stiff, inflexible thumb which is the mark of an intransigent individual. A person with this feature could be prickly to work with and, if it happens to be the manager, then any negotiations or compromises over working conditions or pay settlements might prove difficult to achieve.

Another, most valuable, exercise that the employees can do is a group comparison of their fate lines. Because the fate line gives some pretty strong indications of trends and events that are likely to occur within the working career of the individual, something as important as redundancy would show up clearly on this line. In this case it would be registered by a complete break in the line and so, if this feature should be seen, occurring at the same time in the hands of several people (of course taking into account the age difference of each individual), then a shrewd guess could be made that the company may well run into difficulties around that time. Another shared feature might be a change of direction in the line, again occurring at the same time for each person, and here the markings might suggest a complete change of location for the whole company. These indications, then, would show up well in advance of the actual event taking place and would therefore give the staff plenty of time to consider their future prospects.

Examples of specific professions and occupations

GROCER

Figure 96 is the print of a lady who, for several years, has been running her own successful grocery. The shop itself is run on the lines of fine old tradition and it is a family business where much attention is focused equally on the quality of the goods she sells as well as on the friendly and personal service she

Figure 96

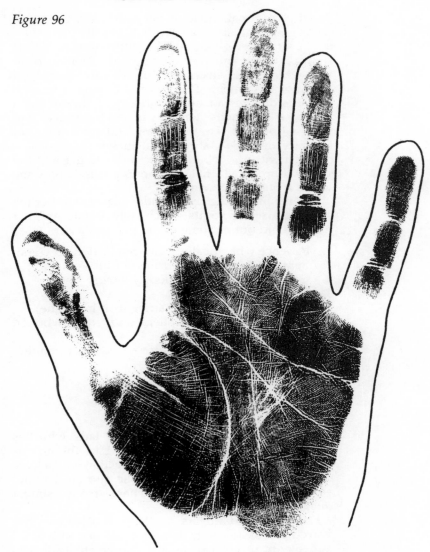

gives to her customers. She was trained in accountancy work which, in her trade, must be an invaluable asset and she has a keen eye for marketing techniques, a skill which she has developed through the years.

Notice the exceptionally long and comparatively straight head line which confirms her logical, practical and mathematical mentality. The palm and fingers are long and lean symbolizing the preference for quality over quantity. The full mount of Venus shows a warm, outward-going and sociable disposition which is so necessary for friendly interaction with her customers. The mount of Luna is low set and this denotes an understanding of rhythms and cycles, a sensitivity which can be translated into intuitive powers. The fine, long and conic finger of Mercury denotes a shrewd businesswoman which, coupled with the whorl on the index finger and the strong thumb, tells that she knows precisely how she wants a business to run.

When considering the qualities required in her job she made seven points which, when analysing her hand, stand out as some of her greatest assets:

1. Patience when dealing with public (long fingers).
2. Sense of humour/cheerfulness (full Venus).
3. Communication skills (long Mercury finger).
4. Stamina (strong hand).
5. Head for figures (long, straightish head line).
6. Toughness with suppliers and staff (whorled index, strong thumb).
7. Advanced insight of future consumer requirements (Luna mount).

HAIRDRESSER

Figure 97 is the print of a creative lady who has turned her talents to hairdressing. Like the grocer, her livelihood depends on her interaction with a large cross-section of the general public and so it is not surprising that they both share many similar qualities.

Her palm and fingers are long and lean with a bowed percussion edge denoting patience with detail and plenty of creative talent. The creativity is also emphasized by the marked curve in the head line. The lower joints on all the fingers are pronounced thus highlighting a strong sense of precision in her work coupled with a need for a tidy working environment. The mounts of Venus, Luna and, in particular, Mercury are all full denoting a social,

Figure 97

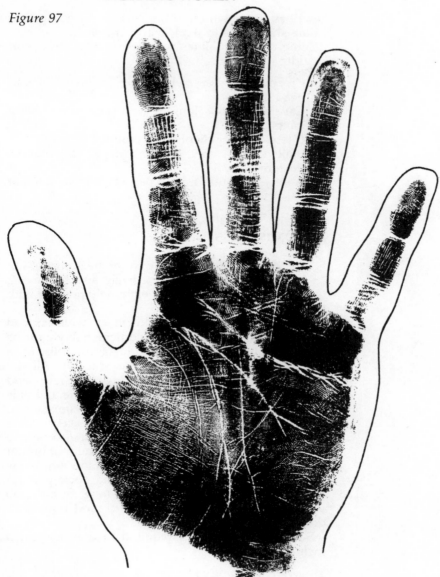

gregarious, warm and chatty disposition, whilst the fullness of all the mounts at the base of the palm tells of a goodly amount of physical strength. Finally, the sharp angle made by the joint at the base of the thumb is known as the angle of manual dexterity and

117

describes a lady who is at her best in any occupation where she is able to work with her hands.

Some of the qualities required in her profession include:

1. Creative eye for style (bowed percussion and head line).
2. Care with detail (long fingers, pronounced basal joints).
3. Interest in her clients (full mounts).
4. Skilled with her hands (angle of manual dexterity).
5. Ability to stand for long periods, (strong palm at base).

HEADMISTRESS

Figure 98 is a print belonging to the headmistress of an infant's school. She has a lively and fun-loving disposition which makes her extremely popular with the children in her care.

The fingers here are held in a wide spread suggesting an open, extroverted personality and the very large mount of Venus instantly tells of a tremendous amount of love and warmth. All the fingerprints are loops indicating a lively and stimulating disposition, one that is flexible and able to bend and flow with changing circumstances. Above all, this highlights a need for variety in her working life and a love of always having to be one jump ahead. The oblique line on the mount of Jupiter tells of insight into the human condition whilst the large mount itself denotes a strong socio-political awareness. The straight index and long, firm thumb indicate strength of character and good powers of discipline and control.

Some of the qualities required in this profession include:

1. Understanding of people (Jupiter mount).
2. Ability to delegate (index finger).
3. Qualities of leadership (strong thumb and index).
4. Tact (slightly waisted thumb).
5. Love of children (full Venus).

Figure 98

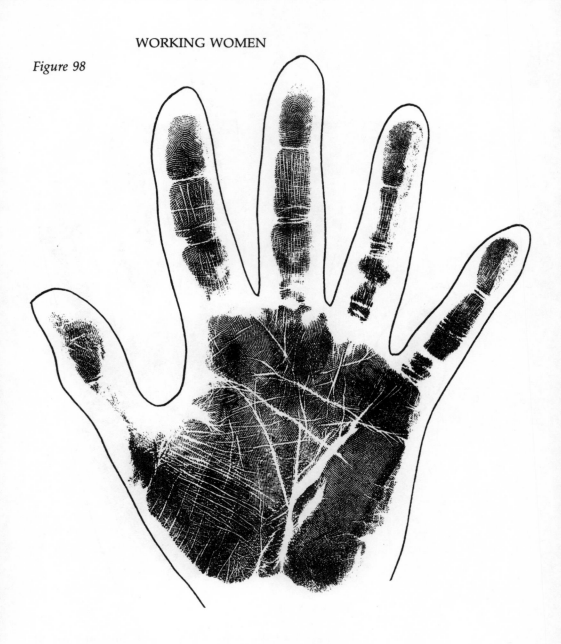

6. Enthusiasm (wide spread fingers).
7. *Joie de vivre* (large mount of Venus).

Figure 99

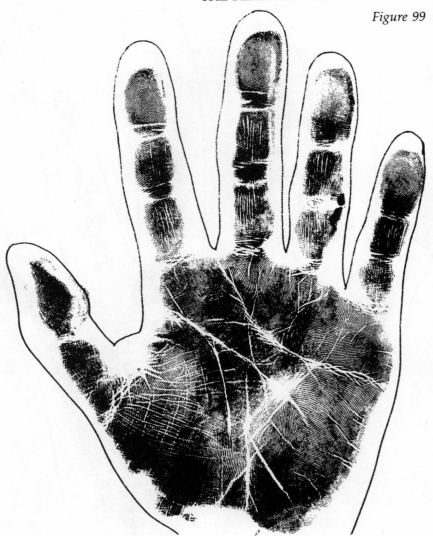

JOURNALIST

Figure 99 is the print of a young and successful journalist working for a weekly newspaper with an extremely large circulation. In her time she has been involved in several scoops, the most recent and dramatic of which was an armed hold-up.

The hand is strong and solid with a long head line which slants downwards across the palm indicating a logical, analytical mind balanced by creative flair. The Mercury finger is fairly long and pointed – always a good clue to literary talents and to 'thinking on one's feet'. The large space between the first and second fingers highlights intellectual independence, that is, she likes to think for herself and draw her own unbiased conclusions to the situations she confronts. Both the Luna and Mercury mounts are pronounced thus illustrating a chatty, warm and sociable personality. The large Jupiter mount tells of a keen socio-political conscience whilst the full mount of Upper Mars shows integrity together with high principles and the courage of her own convictions. Physical courage, too, is illustrated by the full mount of Lower Mars, a quality which must surely be an asset in an occupation that now and again exposes its journalists to potentially dangerous situations.

When considering the essential qualities required in a journalist, several points emerged:

1. Quick witted; quick intelligence (pointed Mercury tip).
2. Social skills – mixing ability (Luna and Mercury mounts).
3. Listening whilst thinking and making judgements (space between first and second fingers).
4. Ability to express oneself factually and clearly (head line, long Mercury finger).
5. Ability to see other people's points of view (mount of Luna).
6. Practical and self-sufficient (strong palm, Lower Mars).

MATRON OF A RESIDENTIAL HOME

Figure 100 is the print of a lady who is the matron of a residential home for the elderly. She has devoted all her life to her medical work, having first trained as an SRN and subsequently working in both private and general practice. She was promoted to matron some years ago – a position which she finds totally fulfilling and rewarding.

Figure 100

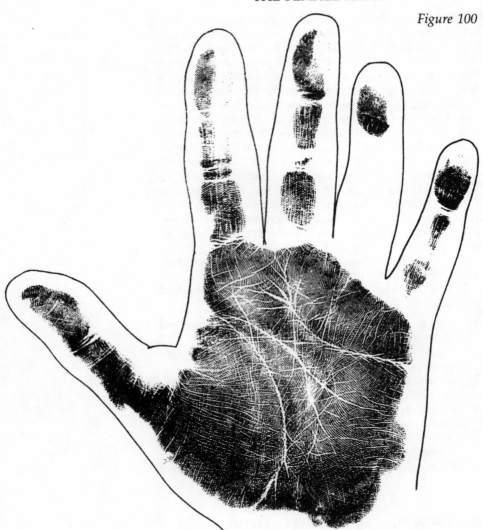

The palm and fingers are strong and capable. The length and thickness of the thumb suggests strength of character and self-assurance whilst the dominant index finger indicates qualities of leadership and command. The head line sweeps across the palm and, despite its undulation, denotes a practical, logical mentality together with great presence of mind. The medical stigmata is present which symbolizes a natural talent for healing and for giving comfort to the sick. The Venus and especially the Luna mounts are full so this lady must be a warm, tolerant and sympathetic person and the loop between the third and fourth fingers illustrates a readiness to see the funny side of any situation. An unusual feature occurs in this hand and that is the ring of Solomon which lies on the index mount encompassing the base of the first finger. This marking illustrates that, through her life and experience, she has gained much wisdom and understanding of people and of the way of the world.

When asked to consider the qualities required in her profession she spontaneously replied:

1. Patience and understanding (basal mounts, ring of Solomon).
2. Sense of humour (skin loop below third and fourth fingers).
3. Practicality (strong palms, straightish head line).
4. No squeamishness (medical stigmata, pragmatic head line).
5. Calm in face of crisis (strong thumbs, head line).

PSYCHOLOGIST

Figure 101 is the print of a senior clinical psychologist. She is highly respected in her field not solely for her professional approach to her work but especially for her high achievement rate when dealing with her patients' problems.

The fingers are all spread out suggesting an open, trusting and enthusiastic disposition. Jupiter is held straight and true signifying a strong sense of justice, honesty and responsibility, and the wide space it forms between itself and its neighbour shows an independent and unbiased mind. The thumb, too, forms a wide angle to the palm and is noticeably flexible which reflects adaptability. Warmth, generosity and a love of mankind are all illustrated by the extremely full and expansive mount of Venus. The Luna mount is low thus highlighting an empathetic nature and a sympathetic ear. Upper Mars is particularly pronounced and this illustrates total

Figure 101

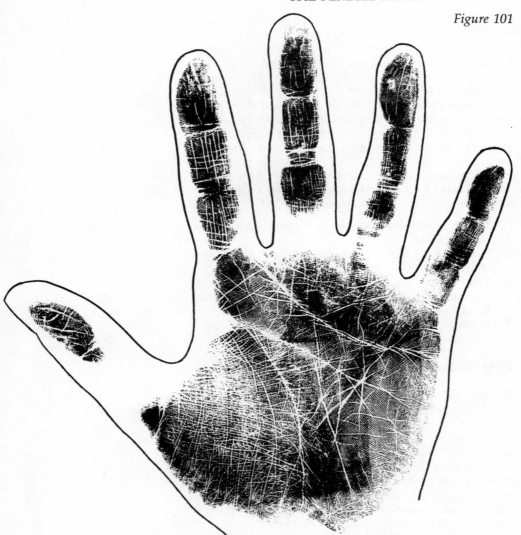

loyalty to her friends, her clients and, most importantly, to her own principles and beliefs.

Some of the qualities required in her profession include:

1. Ability to listen (low mount of Luna).
2. Impartiality (wide spaced index).
3. Open-mindedness (wide angled thumb).

4. Optimism and positive attitude (full Venus mount).
5. Faith and belief in people that they will heal themselves (stance of fingers, upper Mars).

SECRETARY

Figure 102

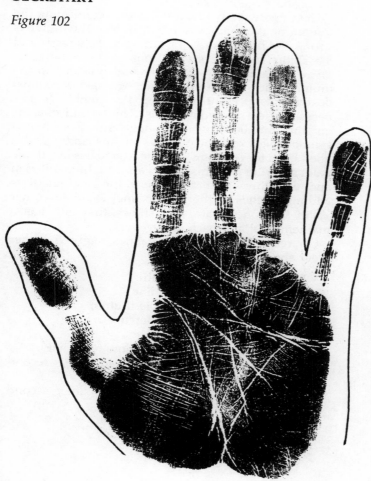

Figure 102 is the print of a personal assistant to the principal of a school. So happy and competent is she in her job that she has held the same position for almost all of her working life. As the secretary, her job is busy and varied and centres around the efficient administration of the school – balancing the books, checking the figures, generally taking the responsibility for the accounts and finances but also for much of the paperwork that links the parents with the school organization.

The fingers are held close together confirming the contentment in her job and way of life. The thumb is strong and flexible showing strength of character and the ability to tackle several jobs at the same time. There's a hint of a waisted second phalanx on the thumb which denotes tact and the angle of manual dexterity is present reflecting the nimble fingers necessary for her typing skills. The second phalanx on the middle finger is long and well-shaped symbolizing excellent qualities of husbandry and a good head for economy. The heart line lies low in the palm showing that this lady is a strong humanitarian and, as it throws out a branch to the head line thus adding touches of the Simian line, it enhances her ability to concentrate and shows that she has a mathematical approach to her work.

On reflecting upon the qualities required in her work she replied:

1. Discretion (waisted thumb).
2. Loyalty (low-lying heart line).
3. Ability to diversify (flexible thumb).
4. Humour (full mount of Mercury).
5. Good memory (head line).
6. Caring (full mount of Luna, low heart line).
7. Knowledge of accounts (head line, second phalanx Saturn).
8. Meticulous record keeping (head line, second phalanx Saturn).

Chapter 6

WIVES AND LOVERS

Hardly a single day goes past without a person interacting with at least one other individual. Each interaction forms the basis of a relationship and the way we relate to others is clearly illustrated in our hands. When you want to find out how you truly feel and why you respond in certain ways to different people then the simplest thing to do is to look at your hands because hand analysis, in fact, is a wonderful mirror of the individual's feelings and emotions.

Are you the quiet passive type in a love affair or do you really do all the running? Do you see marriage as a means to a better social position or to financial security? Is a man for you merely a status symbol or do you treat him as an equal in a partnership? Do you secretly feel superior to men and that you are the real driving force behind the throne? Are you practical, sexy, loving, seductive, easy-going, demanding? What sort of lover do you make? Why do some women divorce several times whilst others find life-long happiness with one partner? All these questions and the happiness, the dangers or the pitfalls that a woman is likely to confront in her relationships, can be answered by a thorough investigation of the hand.

As wives and lovers the first obvious clues lie in the heart line for this is the line that represents our emotions. But, as no one feature in hand analysis can stand on its own, we need also to look at other areas for confirmation, such as the mounts and the percussion edge, for example. When considering compatibility the head and life lines must be examined, and the hand shapes and finger lengths must be taken into account in order to assess the general mentality and disposition of the people concerned. Finally, for the purpose of establishing the actual viability of a relationship, it is to the fate line that we must turn for this will clearly reveal the strengths and weaknesses of that partnership.

THE HEART LINE

The heart line lies horizontally across the palm below the fingers (Figure 103). Where it begins on the hand, and whether it is displaced closer to or further away from the digits, is important as this information gives the basic clues to an individual's emotions. When a woman wants to analyse her own feelings, then, this is where to begin.

On an adult hand the heart line can be measured roughly about 2.5 cm below the middle finger although, of course, variation occurs depending on the actual size of the hand. Unfortunately, only experience or perhaps even a good eye for natural balance can tell at a glance whether the line is higher up or lower down than the norm but 2.5 cm is about average.

The closer the line is situated to the fingers, as seen in Figure 104, the cooler the emotions. This type of woman is logical, rational and analytical when it comes to love and marriage; she seldom lets her emotions run away with her for it is her head that rules her heart – and she hardly ever loses her head! But, should the line be seen much lower down, as in Figure 105, then this is an indication of much warmer emotions, albeit sometimes quite irrational for here it is her heart that rules her head. This lady could never marry solely for money; emotions reign supreme for her and she is often at the mercy of her own feelings, falling in love with complete abandonment and very, very often against her better judgement. The epithet 'love is blind' must have been invented especially for her.

Figure 103

WIVES AND LOVERS

A heart line which is very straight is considered to denote a shrewd and calculative view of love (Figure 106). A lady who possesses this sort of heart line would perhaps consider relationships in a rather dry, matter-of-fact way, uncomplicated by foolish romantic notions. When the line is long and curved (Figure 107) it tells of a fine sense of justice and fair play, so much so that its owner would give others

Figure 105

Figure 104

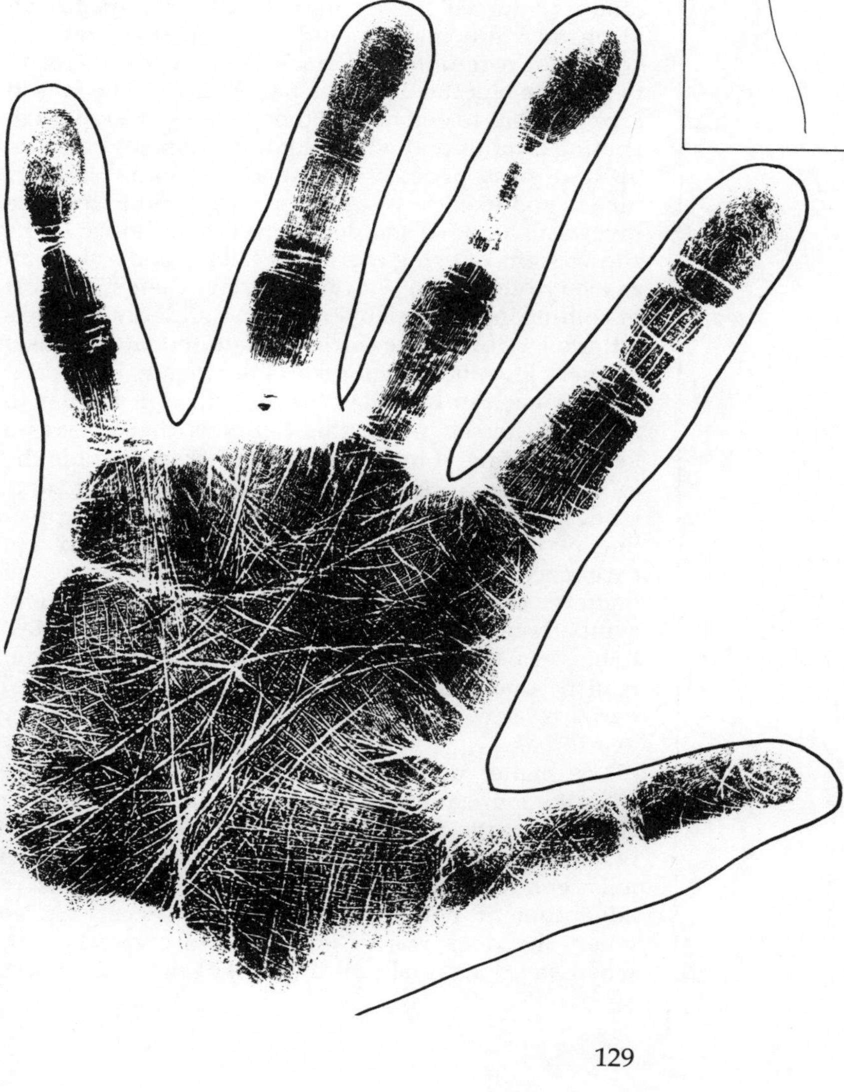

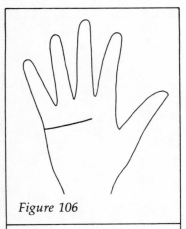

Figure 106

Figure 107

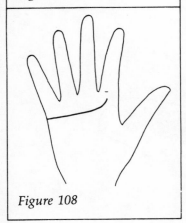

Figure 108

one chance after another to make amends even though she may be let down badly every time. Still she goes on finding excuse after excuse to explain away their behaviour and, more often than not, to her own detriment for she is invariably the one who ends up time and again with egg on her face. This, though, is known as the feminine line and generally tells of a warm, generous and sensitive understanding of human relationships.

A woman whose heart line begins on the index mount (Figure 108) is an eternal romantic. She has an idealistic view of love and relationships and she keeps her rose-tinted spectacles ever at hand, ready to don them at the drop of a hat. The man she falls in love with has to embody all the qualities of a knight in shining armour and when she finds him she sets him up high on a pedestal and worships him. She sees him as god-like, perfect in every way, and in him she invests all her love and devotion. When, however, he shows signs of being mortal, as fallible and as human as every other man with feet of clay, then she is lost in confusion and disillusionment. Suddenly she feels bitterly let down, her world is shattered and it is as if her very love, her devotion and her loyalty have been thrown back in her face. So difficult is it for her to reconcile herself when this happens that it takes a very long time, if indeed ever, for her to rekindle the love that she once felt so passionately for that same man. Perhaps the answer for those with this type of line would be to moderate their standards of excellence or slightly lower their expectations in matters of the heart and become a bit more sympathetic and tolerant when it comes to peoples' foibles. In this way, they would develop a greater realistic understanding of the human condition and perhaps save themselves a lot of unnecessary heartbreak.

The higher up the mount the line creeps (Figure 109), the more ambitious the lady is likely to be in her choice of partner. She needs a lover she can be proud of, that she can look up to and that she considers a jolly good catch. Marriage for her is a means of advancement, perhaps financially and socially too, so when she does marry, she must marry well. But, when she does finally find the right man, she backs him to the hilt, giving total loyalty and devoting herself tirelessly to his success and to the happiness of their marriage.

A forked beginning to the line commencing on or near the index mount often signifies the potential for a happy and harmonious loving partnership (Figure 110). A lady with this line seems to possess a wealth of understanding about people and relationships that makes her tolerant and easy to live with. Such a cheerful and easy-going disposition, then, is an excellent augury for a successful marriage.

When the line runs below the mount almost to the very edge of the palm, (Figure 111), it tells of a person for whom work is extremely important, so much so that at times it may come first, even before relationships. A woman with this feature must make her husband or lover understand this need in her and he must learn to accept her on those terms. Very often, because of her dedication to her work, this is the sort of lady who is to be found on committees, or who is constantly being called upon to shoulder positions of responsibility. For a smooth-running relationship, her lover must be prepared to listen to her troubles about her work and to share the burdens with her. But, if he is not prepared to give her room to pursue her work or chosen career then she is going to feel held back, with no scope for personal growth and development, and the relationship could be badly damaged as a result.

The lady whose heart line begins high up between the first two fingers, (Figure 112), is very warm, loving and soft-hearted. She is extremely practical and down-to-earth in all matters of love, giving generously of herself and her time. She is not, however, verbally demonstrative, for she finds it difficult to put her feelings into words and so she would rather show how much she cares by the little things she does for her partner. Perhaps she might buy him a small present – his favourite chocolate or after-shave – or prepare his favourite meal if she notices that his spirits are low, or yet again she may, though dropping with sleep, sit up with him until the early hours just to keep him company if he's engrossed in his hobby or if he's brought work home to finish. These are, in her way, tokens or gestures of

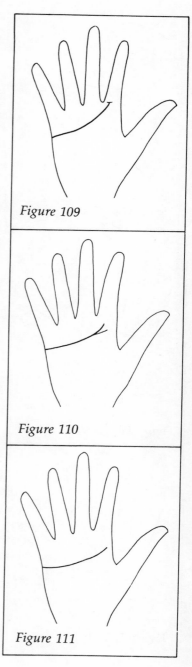

Figure 109

Figure 110

Figure 111

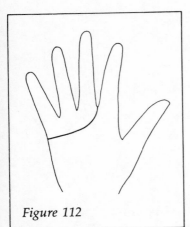

Figure 112

Figure 113

Figure 114

her love for him. But to be able to say readily and spontaneously 'I love you' is so hard for her, as is 'You're getting on my nerves, you louse', that the very words seem to freeze on her lips. And often she will find that, because she can't easily put her feelings into words, then misunderstandings can occur, especially so in the early stages of a relationship. Not only that, but her inability to express her innermost thoughts, both the positive and negative ones, can also lead to bottling up and repressing those feelings and she can end up becoming very frustrated indeed. So for her own sanity and well-being she should try to find an outlet for her feelings – confiding in a close friend or keeping a diary, for example, or writing little notes or letters to her sweetheart – and in this way she can clear the air.

The sign of the pure sensualist, it is said, is a short, straight heart line which begins directly beneath the second finger (Figure 113). This lady can string along several men at the same time, enjoying one night stands and sex for the sheer glorious hell of it! Don't expect her to get too serious either for she's a fickle, flirtatious type; but she certainly enjoys herself and she makes sure she has plenty of fun!

If this shorter line, instead of being straight, curves deeply up towards the second finger, as in Figure 114, it may denote a more masculine approach to sex which, on a lady's hand, could imply lesbian or bisexual tendencies.

On a few hands a rather unusual form of the heart line occurs which is known as the Simian line (Figure 115). It lies almost a third of the way down the palm and incorporates both the head and heart lines into one horizontal groove which stretches right across from edge to edge. The presence of this line always denotes intensity, especially so where the emotions are concerned. The owner of this line would throw herself heart and soul into a relationship, loving deeply and to the exclusion of all else. Because her love is so intense she expects to be loved back with the same depth of passion, with the same concentration and focus of attention. Extreme jealousy is her greatest fault especially during her early years and particularly so if both hands sport the

Simian line. If, however, she has the line on one hand only, then the jealousy and intensity of emotion modifies and mellows with age, especially once she is past her mid-thirties.

Traditionally, it is said that the best line to possess is one which has a triple fork, one branch across, one on the index mount and one between the first two fingers (Figure 116). A woman with this line would be graced with all the warmth, passion, romantic idealism and common sense – the ingredients that should lead to a happy and healthy loving relationship.

Figure 116

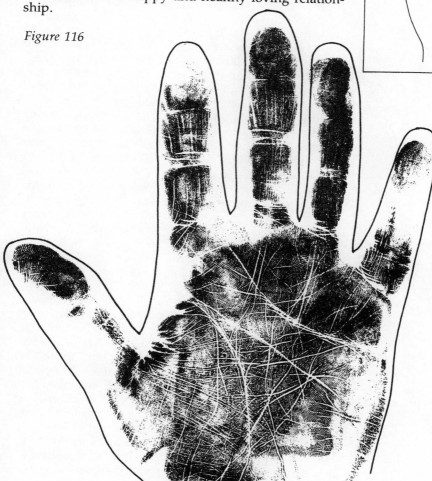

Figure 115

Right- and left-handedness

Analysing emotions becomes even more fascinating when the heart line on one hand does not match the heart line on the other. The functions corresponding to the right and left hands are quite discrete so any variation in the two lines will naturally manifest itself in a discrepancy between the way a woman feels deep inside and the way she appears emotionally to the rest of the world. When such a discrepancy as this exists it can indeed explain why misunderstandings seem to crop up all the time or why her relationships just don't run smoothly. Whereas previously it might have been quite hard for her to work out why things kept on going wrong, and she might even have always put the blame on the other person involved, now, by understanding this dichotomy in her hands, she will be able to change her behaviour in order to take such inconsistencies into account.

On a right-handed person, the markings on that hand represent the persona, the way she behaves in public, the picture she presents to other people. Her left hand, though, reveals her private self, her instincts and her inner being. On a left-hander this rule is simply reversed. It is by interpreting each line in turn, according to whether it is on the right or left, that the full picture of a woman's emotions slowly emerges. So let us take as an example the hypothetical case of a right-handed lady whose right heart line travels across the palm beneath the first finger whilst that on her left begins on the index mount (see Figure 117).

The line on this lady's left hand, then, would suggest that she is a romantic and she sees her man as a hero type and her love affair with him like something straight out of a Mills and Boon novel. This is how she perceives herself but, in reality though, her right heart line reveals that, in the eyes of her lover, she is a fairly independent, self-sufficient person whose work comes first and relationships later. She secretly would love to be swept off her feet, clothed from head to foot in shimmering tulle whilst he runs through his Rudolf Valentino act just for her. He, however, seeing her as the efficient career-type, believes that any sign of 'romantic nonsense' on his

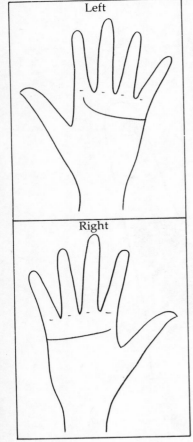

Figure 117

134

part would render him so low in her estimation that he might as well disappear altogether. So he responds to that image she presents by being cool, capable, practical and competent. She, through her romantic eyes, can't understand why he's always so distant – perhaps, after all, she argues, he doesn't love her at all. An interpretation of her heart lines would soon sort it out and put her right!

THE MOUNTS

Having studied the lines, the next features to analyse are the mounts and, with the question of love and marriage in mind, those of Venus and Luna are particularly relevant.

The Mount of Venus is located at the base of the thumb and is encircled by the life line (Figure 118). This area represents one's love of life and enthusiasm for living. For best indications, the mount should be firm but springy, well-rounded and stretching out to almost the centre of the palm. With this formation, the mount represents an easy-going nature and a loving temperament. A woman with a full mount of Venus radiates warmth and generosity; she attracts people easily to her for she possesses a certain *ésprit* or charisma, and one feels that in her there is almost a hunger for living life to the full, for giving love and receiving it. The fullness of the mount also equates with virility, so a well-rounded area here would suggest a passionate lady with a good, healthy appetite for sex.

Figure 118

If this mount is thin, rather meagre in appearance and contained within a life line which hugs closely around the thumb then the lady concerned is likely to be somewhat cool and reserved (Figure 119). She can seem distant, keeping herself to herself, almost supercilious and certainly critical. She lacks robustness, and is possibly pale-looking and fragile in appearance. Approaching her can initially be difficult for she doesn't exactly spill over with loving kindness, so making the first move is the tricky part in forming a relationship with her. Once the ice has been broken, though, the full extent of her personality can then be explored and she may indeed

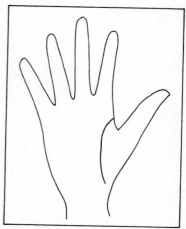

Figure 119

show that she's not quite such a cold fish as she at first appeared.

If this mount feels flabby to the touch it often reveals the sensualist – someone who likes to live in the lap of luxury, in an easy, indolent sort of way, enjoying all the pleasures of the senses.

At the opposite side of the palm lies the Mount of Luna (Figure 120). When this area, which is located just above the wrist at the edge of the palm, is full and well-defined it denotes sensitivity. A lady with this part of the hand well developed has sympathy and depth of understanding; she can read between the lines and is highly receptive to people's moods. She doesn't find it at all difficult to put herself in their shoes or to empathize with them and consequently she naturally draws people who find that she has a soft and warm shoulder to cry on. Because of her intuition, she is able to read her lover like a book so any dissembling on his part is instantly uncovered. If he is loving and honest, however, he will find in her a wonderfully receptive soul-mate, someone who is prepared to understand him – warts and all.

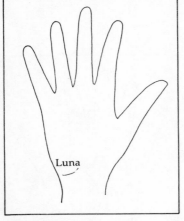

Figure 120

COMPATIBILITY CHECKS

Before even considering a romantic liaison a good comparison of the two pairs of hands will yield an invaluable amount of information about the sort of relationship the two people are likely to have together. Will it be stormy, mutually caring, destructive, explosive, creative, great fun? Will it end in true love, marriage or divorce? Will the two people involved feel trapped and frustrated or will there be room for each to grow and develop within the partnership?

Heart Lines. Firstly, compare each heart line in turn. Decide which type the individuals possess. If they are alike then both people will share the same emotions and each will understand how the other feels. If the lines are so different as to suggest that the two people will never see eye to eye emotionally, then a choice has to be made: is the relationship worth continuing, worth fighting for, or should they cut their losses now before the going gets too tough?

If they decide that the relationship is strong and worth trying to make a success, then they shouldn't despair at this stage because there are other factors seen in the hand which help to mitigate against this emotional disparity. The head lines may show similarities so that, although they may not *feel* in the same way, they do, nevertheless, *think* in the same way. With a marriage of minds they would be able to overcome the rest. Or perhaps their hand shapes are of the same type so at least they share the same basic disposition, and therefore interests.

Whether the heart lines match or not, because of the very nature of a relationship where two separate egos come together, the insight that is given by actually identifying and defining the way each one feels must surely help to focus attention on the way each interacts with the other. Such an understanding must usefully clarify the emotional issues within that relationship and thereby help to strengthen it.

Head Lines. Having analysed the heart lines the next thing to do is to compare and contrast the head lines. This line represents the intellect and will give strong clues about the way each partner thinks in life. The basic difference in mental approach is between a straight line or a curved one. Should the lines match, then the couple will think alike but, if they differ, this may not in any way be detrimental, for each would be able to offer a way of looking at life that the other might otherwise have missed altogether. But, of course, there is also here the possiblity that a dissimilarity in the way of thinking could lead to an inability to come to terms with each other's point of view! Again, a little understanding of the way each mind works must surely lead to greater tolerance and acceptance and thus to a more harmonious life together.

Someone whose head line lies straight across the palm is basically practical, logical, analytical, pragmatic or has the sort of mind that thinks in 'straight lines'. This line is often attributed to scientists, mathematicians, technologists or anyone with a basically practical way of thinking about the world.

A curved line denotes an artistic, imaginative or inventive mentality. Anything to do with the arts, languages, or divergent creativity is suggested by this line. If the curve is very steep or penetrates deeply into the mount of Luna then the imagination can be so rich that it often carries the individual away. Moodiness, a strong sense of nostalgia and swings of highs and lows are often characterized by this line.

A line which begins straight and then curves shows someone who enjoys a mentality which is a combination of both analysis and creativity.

The Fingers. The information revealed by the length and spread of the fingers must next be superimposed upon that gleaned from the lines. Long fingers denote someone who likes detail, who has plenty of patience and who needs time to process information. Short fingers, though, are inspirational. They are quick at catching on and dislike detail for it slows them down. They make excellent planners for they have the ability to take an overall view rather than get drawn by minutiae. If a short-fingered woman, for example, is married to a long-fingered man, she may find that there are times when his pedantic insistence on precision simply drives her mad. He, in his turn, can become rather irritated by her cavalier attitude to anything which requires steady application and complete concentration. Harmony, though, can be achieved if they both acknowledge their limitations and work within them together – she, laying the broad plans; he, filling in the details.

Fingers and thumbs which spread out widely when the hand is placed comfortably on the table, illustrate someone who is flexible, open, frank, generous and outgoing. When, however, all the digits are held close together, it signifies a person who tends to be reticent, perhaps with fixed ideas, rather controlled and even secretive.

Hand Shapes. The shape of the hand lays down the fundamental character and disposition of the individual. There are some shapes which work well together whilst others would simply not be able to agree with another person's principles, philosophy or way of life. The basic hand shapes are the square, the conic, the spatulate and the psychic.

The square hand belongs to the hard worker. These people are practical, sensible and down-to-earth. They are earthy and often materialistic types who like to have a fixed routine in their lives and consequently have little time for airy-fairy notions or theories. The outdoor life suits them and if they are not surrounded by a pastoral or rural setting then they are likely to devote much time to cultivating their gardens or taking long, brisk walks in the countryside. The square hand would, of course, get along well with its own kind. With the conic, it might be a hit-and-miss affair. The conic's flexibility could enliven the square, and the square could impart a sense of solidity to the other. The spatulate would be a much better proposition for the square as they are both highly charged with energy. But the psychic would be just asking for trouble. With this relationship they would never see eye to eye – one is earthy whilst the other is ethereal, one is concrete and the other a dreamer, one is practical but the other is quite unrealistic.

The conic hand is creative and artisitic. These people need plenty of variety in their lives and make excellent organizers. They can work quickly and instinctively, often letting their intuition guide them. Flexibility is one of their outstanding characteristics and they love nothing better than getting their teeth into a good challenge in life. Two conics together would certainly be stimulating company for each other. With the square, life might be somewhat dull at times although the versatility of the conic might be able to find ways of breathing life into the situation. The spatulate would make a good match for the conic as both have plenty of enthusiasm and many interests in life. A partnership with the psychic type could work for they both have in common a love of art and a creative flair.

The spatulate hand is characterized by mental and physical energy. As thinkers, these people have a flair for invention and innovation; as doers, they are invariably sports-orientated. Men and women of ideas, explorers, inventors, discoverers, restless in their quest to further their knowledge or to unearth the unknown: this is how the spatulate type has often been described. Two people who both have the spatulate hand would make a restless, untiring and mutually stimulating couple. The square would be able to keep up with the pace of the spatulate and also provide a solid and stable background. The conic would make a good companion for the spatulate but the psychic probably would not.

The psychic hand denotes an eye for aesthetics, refined tastes and a sensitive disposition. Because of their sensitivity people with pyschic hands are sometimes nervous and a little highly-strung, as well as impressionable and with a tendency to live with their heads in the clouds. They're not at all worldly-wise but more impractical and unrealistic when it comes to the nitty-gritty of everyday life. But these people do make excellent artists and poets. Two psychics would probably make wonderful music together, in every sense of the word. They would, more often than not, be completely oblivious to the harsher realities of life and how well they would cope might perhaps depend on such vagaries as their financial situation, for example. With a square-handed partner life for a psychic would probably be quite intolerable – they're like chalk and cheese! A conic could be fairly compatible, a spatulate wouldn't.

INDICATIONS OF MARRIAGE

The point at which two people decide to get married, set up home or start living together, on a fairly permanent basis, is often clearly represented on the hand. The best indications for this are seen on the fate line and Chapter 10 explains how to measure time on this line so that the likelihood of the actual event can be dated.

The classical interpretation of marriage is seen when a branch from the percussion edge actually merges into the fate line proper (Figure 121). Nowadays, however, this could just as well be interpreted as the point at which a couple decide to commit themselves to each other, to start living together or set up home together on a fairly permanent basis. Careful analysis of the branch and also of the structure of the fate line before and after the merger will reveal much about the nature of the

Figure 121

relationship and the subsequent commitment or marriage.

If the branch is in any way broken (Figure 122a), islanded (Figure 122b) or has tiny bars through it (Figure 122c) then it would show that the relationship had a rather stormy beginning. If the branch is broken, it indicates an on-off affair; if islanded, the relationship is filled with problems and anxieties; if shot through with bars, then it is subjected to outside opposition or interference.

If, at the merger, both the branch and the fate line thicken and strengthen this is a splendid sign that the marriage will be beneficial to both parties concerned. But, if the fate line should show signs of weakening, islanding or fragmenting (Figure 123a), it warns that trouble and problems loom ahead for that couple. Any sign of the structure weakening suggests frustration and an underlying unrest. Fragmentation of the line could indicate several changes, perhaps for the worse, connected with their lifestyle, financial situation or career. Islands would then denote the subsequent worries and anxieties brought about by this situation.

When these sorts of indications occur, the rest of the hand should be carefully analysed in order to detect any other factors which might have a direct bearing on the situation. Check the head line, for instance, to see if the individual is going through a period of personal crisis. The presence of trauma lines might perhaps suggest parental pressure as the root cause of the disquiet.

Another interesting observation is when these adverse markings are seen only on one partner's hands whilst the other's remain perfectly unobstructed. This would indicate that the marriage has detrimentally affected only one person, causing him or her to have serious doubts and to feel uneasy, whereas the other remains quite contented and oblivious to any undercurrents of impending unrest. When, however, the fate line regains its strength and direction (Figure 123b), it tells that the problems have been resolved and that a new stability has been reached.

If the branch, proceeding from the percussion edge towards the centre, fails to meet the fate line (Figure

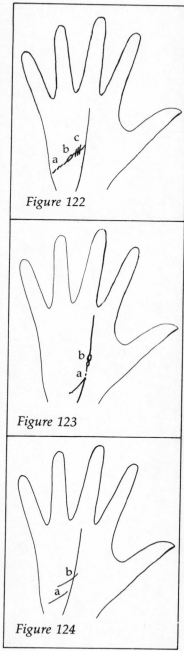

Figure 122

Figure 123

Figure 124

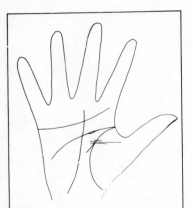

Figure 125

Figure 126

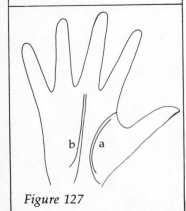

Figure 127

124a), it implies that the relationship will not last. But if the branch does hit the fate line and, instead of merging with it, actually crosses over it (Figure 124b), this is an indication that the very marriage itself will be called off, perhaps even at the last moment.

Signs of break-up and divorce are seen in a variety of ways and a little bit of detective work around the hand is required to put all the facts together. Deeply etched trauma lines are some of the first giveaways of emotional problems although, of course, these may well occur for many different reasons other than marital breakdown. However, this is as good a place to start as any. If the trauma line is accompanied by a break on the fate line, or perhaps by a travel line on the life line, then a change of lifestyle is indicated. There may also be an island on the head line, denoting worry, or even a new section of head line altogether showing a complete change of mental orientation or new intellectual stance.

Figure 125 illustrates all these indications occurring on a hand at the same time. But again, it must be stressed that any, or indeed all, of these factors being present on the hand need not signify the breakdown of a marriage. They could just as easily suggest several other situations which would result in the same amount of mental and emotional upheaval. That is why careful and thorough investigation must be carried out into all the circumstances leading up to these events in order to satisfy one's mind that the signs do indeed denote a separation. The irretrievable breakdown of a marriage does not happen in a vacuum, nor does it occur overnight, so there have to be a series of prior events marked on the hand which give clues to the build-up of unhappiness and the slow erosion of love within the relationship. It is all these clues put together that ultimately paint the picture of separation or divorce.

The death of a much-loved partner may sometimes be indicated on the hand by a long line, starting from the percussion edge just beneath the little finger, travelling across below the ring finger and then dipping to cut through the heart, fate and maybe even the head lines (Figure 126). Such an event would naturally leave behind it devastating consequences which would be marked elsewhere on the hand, either on the head, fate, life or Apollo lines, in the forms of breaks, crossing bars or islands.

A line, springing from the inside of the life line and thereafter running parallel to it (Figure 127a) can denote the sort of spouse who is not so much a partner but a very close soul-mate. Another sign of an excellent match is seen when a branch, again from the percussion edge, travels towards the fate line but, instead of meeting it, rises up and takes on a parallel course beside it (Figure 127b). Here, the union is not only a good relationship but a first-class partnership too.

When analysing the whole question of love and marriage, both partners' hands should be compared firstly to ascertain compatibility and then secondly, to establish similarity and synchronicity of events between them. If they consistently show indications of the same sort of events occurring roughly at the same times – like moves, emotional upheavals or the births of babies for example – then it is highly probable that the two people will spend the rest of their lives together.

Finally, it must never be forgotten that people have free wills and that lines on the hands can, and frequently do, change so that we are not necessarily stuck forever with the same indications. The hand is merely a representation of ourselves, a map, a guide of our lives. We have the power to control, to choose, to make decisions of our own and in this way we can blindly accept, reject as far as possible or at least learn to skirt around those events that are indicated in our hands.

Should a woman embarking on a new relationship detect on her hands warnings of future problems within that partnership, then she has a much better chance of dealing with them well before they ever rear their ugly heads, and she may even be able to avoid their occurrence altogether. If she sees from the start that the union is likely to be quite disastrous then she will have time to pull out before investing too much of herself and thereby avoid becoming deeply wounded. But if, conversely, the relationship does at first appear precarious and fraught with difficulties although it may have many positive attributes, a look at the more promising future trends in her hands might give her just the necessary encouragement she needs to stick it out and to fight for its eventual success. In this way, rather than reject the affair altogether, she will be able to turn a stormy and turbulent relationship into a strong and mutually fulfilling partnership.

Chapter 7

MOTHERS AND CHILDREN

Giving birth is probably the most significant event in any woman's life. The process takes almost a year to complete and its results have far-reaching consequences which last for the rest of her days. Motherhood, however it may be considered, is not an easy job. Historically, it has been depicted in beatific terms and described variously as a fulfilling, rewarding, mystical, even holy experience. Today, however, we tend to be more honest about the role of a mother and we view its virtues with greater realism.

Bearing and rearing children can be a drain on our physical, emotional and economic resources. They force us to change our habits, to question our beliefs, to become accountable and assume responsibility. Of course, the rewards are there too – the rays of sunshine, unannounced and unexpected, filter through the daily routines; our children disarm us with their innocence, their beauty and their joy. But few would deny that in reality the work the children bring us is constant and hard – from that thin cry in the dead of night that breaks into our precious sleep to the painful emotional metamorphosis of the child from adolescence into adult life and beyond.

Sometimes we can help, take part, support or intervene; we can guide, chastise, counsel or cajole. But sometimes we can only watch from the wings. We must step back and give them their freedom to grow, to explore, to develop in their own right, and hope that everything we have invested of ourselves in them, of our experiences, of our mistakes, of our wisdom and our love will help them, no matter how minutely, to cope just that little bit better with their own lives.

As with all other facets of life, an understanding of the basic principles of hand analysis can be invaluable in the infinite complexities of being a mother. At the very outset, indications in our hands will give us a pretty good idea of when we are likely to have children. Any predispositon to gynaecological complications may also be interpreted here. So at least with this knowledge one is able to make certain predictions, to prepare oneself and take control rather than be caught unawares.

Later, by analysing our children's hands we can gain a much clearer picture of their characters, their strengths and weaknesses, likes and dislikes. Understanding their hands means that we as mothers will be able to give better guidance when it comes to their abilities or choice of careers. Relationships, too, should run smoother, not only within the family, but also with friends and acquaintances. And all the time we will be able to monitor their growth and keep abreast of the rapid physical and psychological changes that take place throughout the course of their development.

ENVIRONMENT VERSUS HEREDITY

The old argument of nature versus nurture, whether an individual is primarily influenced by environment or made up solely of inherited characteristics, is a deep and fascinating issue. The study of the hand certainly confirms that many similarities are passed down from one generation to another, for the hand shape often runs in families and so do the skin markings. This suggests then that, just as the colour of the eyes or hair, or the shape of the nose or fullness of the mouth are inherited, so too are dispositional traits or basic character or temperamental tendencies. Interestingly, many of the lines are also repeated amongst various members of the same family so that,

Figure 128a and b

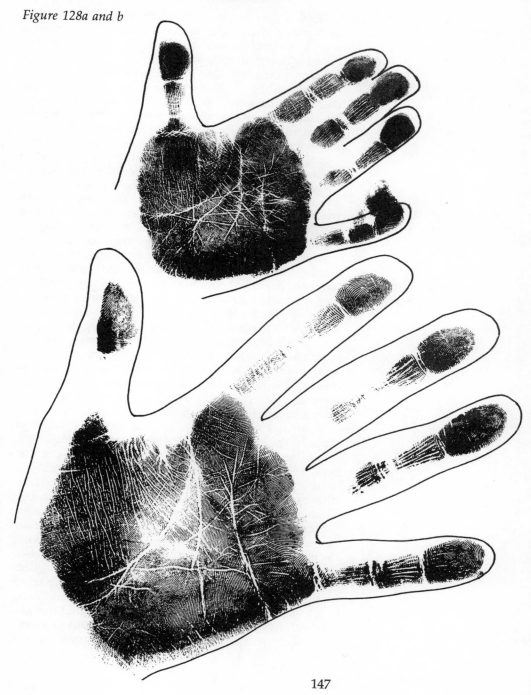

as a result, a child may indeed resemble her mother in the way she thinks and acts but, in fact, when it comes to emotions, she might take after her grandfather, for example.

Figures 128a and 128b are the prints of a 26-year-old mother and her 3-year-old daughter. Many similarities exist between the two. Both share the same basically conic-shaped palm and practical fingers. The head lines follow a similar path even as far as the development of the fork at the end, the life lines sweep out into a generous curve and the forked heart lines are both situated between the index and Saturn fingers. So it shows that they are both lively, creative but also practical types. Intellectually they are both imaginative and emotionally warm and loving but perhaps not verbally expressive of their feelings – they both tend to bottle things up. But there are obvious differences too. The child's thumb is much stronger than that of her mother, her life and head lines are not attached for such a long distance and the fate line is longer and more evident from a younger age. All this adds up to a stronger character in the youngster, greater will-power and an altogether more independent nature. Perhaps then, these may be qualities she has inherited from her father or grandparents. A very interesting study could be made of a family tree of hand prints whereby the various elements and characteristics could be traced down through the generations.

These two prints then, would certainly seem to uphold the heredity part of the argument although it must be emphasized that whilst each characteristic may be shared with various members of the family, it is the particular combination of these characteristics that makes each person a unique individual. The fact that lines change, however, that important differences occur between right and left hands and that some of the indications suggest only predispositions as opposed to irrevocable outcome, must surely lend weight to the opposite side of the argument – that environmental factors do indeed have a large part to play in shaping and influencing an individual.

Lines can, and do, change and some quite quickly at that. Incidental lines like those which denote stress on the fingertips may appear and disappear over a matter of weeks or months. Changes within the major lines are seen, too, for they may grow or contract in length, islands or trauma lines might develop, or the lines could break or fray. Consider a head line, for example, which over a year or so lengthens by something like a centimetre. This would show that the subject is in a situation where she is learning and developing and expanding her mind to a remarkable degree. If, as in many cases, this line then grows longer than the one on her subjective hand it would indicate that she has intellectually developed herself further than her limited inherited 'lot' might otherwise have allowed.

And then again, certain indications of predisposition are also seen in the hand – a susceptibility to a particular disorder, say, or perhaps a latent flair for music. With judicious care that susceptibility need not develop into chronic disease and, equally, if not exposed to the right environment that musical talent could lie dormant forever.

Figures 129a and 129b are two prints of the same hand taken at an interval of eight years. Notice the changes that have taken place between the two, the more recent one (Figure 129b) showing a greater amount of activity than the former one (Figure 129a). Certainly there are several differences, the most important of which is the development of the head line, illustrating intellectual growth and expansion. Other discrepancies include the lengthening of the fate line together with the strengthening of the Sun line which both indicate a greater degree of control and a more positive attitude to the individual's way of life and her picture of the future. One special feature which stands as important evidence to the fact that we all have the power to control our own destinies is the island which occurs in Figure 129a about three-quarters of the way down the life line and, as such, shows the possibility of ill health somewhere around the age of fifty. But, in Figure 129b the island has completely disappeared showing that the individual has managed, whether through a change in her way of life, through diet, preventive medicine, or whatever, to prevent that particular situation from developing at that time in her life.

There can only be one conclusion to this argument,

Figure 129a

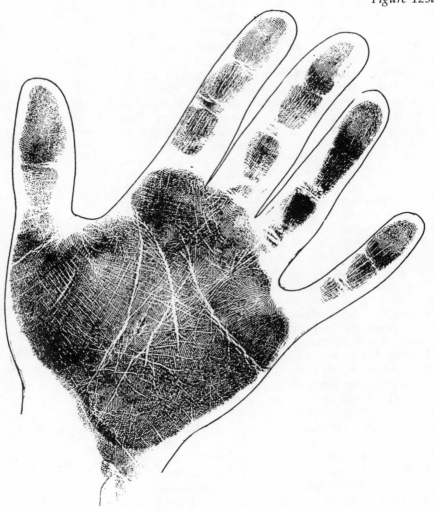

then, that we are indeed 'genetically programmed', but that environmental influences play just as large a part in shaping our lives because without the right exposure or cues to trigger us off then many of our inherited characteristics, positive or negative, may never develop at all.

Figure 129b

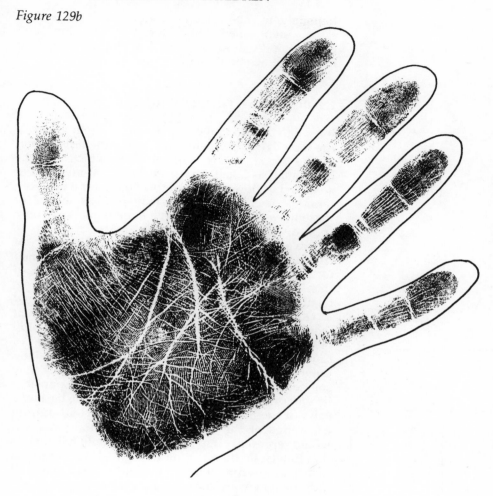

The importance of this argument from a mother's point of view is that, just as she herself is made up of lots of little characteristics handed down to her from this ancestor or that, so too will the 'jigsaw' that is her child be composed of thousands of pieces and the pattern it makes will be totally individualistic. Some of these characteristics will be good and some may be bad but by recognizing them, through studying the hand, she may be able, if she chooses, to furnish the right environment in which to develop and encourage the desirable ones and help to prevent or negate the negative ones.

INDICATIONS OF OFFSPRING

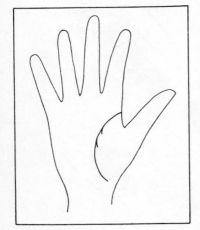

Figure 130

It used to be said that one's children were marked on the top edge of the palm, just below the little finger, in the form of tiny vertical lines which cut the horizontal so-called 'marriage lines'. Modern hand analysis has now disproved this notion for it has been found that childless ladies may possess several of these lines whilst some with a large family may only sport one or two.

Nowadays, when looking for indications of children it is the life line which is carefully examined for clues. Tiny branches which drop off the inside of this line, as depicted in Figure 130, denote relationships or influences which may be interpreted as children. When this is the case, the very point at which the branch separates itself from the main body of the life line denotes the time of birth. A word of caution though – care should be taken when making judgements about these tiny offshoots as they may sometimes represent a new dependent or responsibility entering the subject's life rather than the birth of a baby. If the branch appears within the child-bearing age range of the individual then in most cases it would represent offspring, but if it should fall outside that time scale then greater thought should be given to its true interpretation. In the latter case it may well indicate a new affection for a close niece or nephew. Equally, it might suggest step- or foster-children or even, perhaps, the acquisition of a new and greatly loved pet.

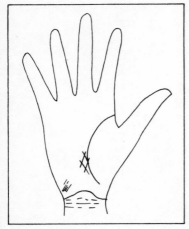

Figure 131

A susceptibility to either difficulties or problems connected with the reproductive cycle, ranging from irregularities in menstruation to possible complications in giving birth, may sometimes be seen by a triangular or diamond-shaped formation located about two-thirds of the way down the life line, as illustrated in Figure 131. This is further confirmed if the top rascette (bracelet) around the wrist arches upwards into the palm itself, or if a group of lines are seen obliquely on the base of the Luna mount just above the wrist. The existence of such a feature does not categorically state that gynaecological trouble looms ahead, it merely points to a possible predisposition to these problems, which with care and constant monitoring may be controlled or circumvented altogether.

CHILDREN'S HANDS

Being able to analyse the hand of a child has many obvious advantages. The first benefit is that, by a simple glance at the shape, a mother can size up the character of her child with great ease. Most parents would contend that they understand their children anyway without having to resort to hand analysis. But do they really? Parents are notoriously subjective when it comes to assessing their own children and can so easily develop blind spots when confronting certain difficult issues. What hand analysis provides is an independent, objective measure which, used correctly, can be startlingly accurate and unbiased.

Before attempting to analyse her child's hand, a mother should consider several important points. Firstly, her child's hand will grow and with development will come change. She must remember, therefore, that the patterns are not fixed and that a flexible attitude should be taken to the indications shown. Secondly, having assessed the various gifts and talents, she should remember to allow these to develop in their own time. Each child is unique and develops at his or her own rate. To push or to shape that little individual before his or her own time could do untold damage for the future. So the mother should try to provide the right environment in which those talents can emerge and flower without too much interference. Thirdly, each child has free-will just as an adult does. He or she may not choose, for whatever reason, to follow a particular indication shown in his or her hand. To force that child, because the mother thinks she may know best, could unleash consequences that would have their repercussions for many years to come.

It is important, then, that when assessing her children's hands the mother should be aware of the new power that she will gain and that power should be looked upon with great respect and only used with wisdom. When it comes to children, everything about hand analysis indicates that they must not be forced into a mould but given plenty of gentle advice and guidance together with the right atmosphere of positive encouragement in which to develop and mature at their own pace and in their own way.

Finally, the mother should try to constantly remind herself of her own relationship with, and attitude to, her children. By checking her own heart line she will be able to confirm her own dreams, ambitions and expectations of her children. Does she have high standards and will her offspring be constantly challenged to meet them? Will she, though deeply loving, be unable to express that love verbally? Or does she have over-romanticized ideas about them and thus over-inflate their abilities and capabilities? Before attempting any analysis of her children's hands, she must try to examine her own position first and with honesty evaluate herself and her feelings because in this way she will be able to bring a greater degree of objectivity to the whole situation.

So, by categorizing the shape of the child's hands the first step towards establishing his or her character can be made. Chapter 2 describes hand and finger shapes but a quick résumé is listed below. The shape of the palm and fingers determines the basic character of the child and the lines will supply information on the physical, emotional and mental attitudes to life.

Palm shapes

Youngsters with square palms are basically hard-working, solid even stolid types (Figure 132). Routine is important to them and they may find changes difficult to accept. They like to work in a systematic fashion usually preferring practical or technological subjects to the imaginative or artisitic ones.

Children with conic palms can be extremely imaginative and creative (Figure 133). They need many interests to hold their attention for variety

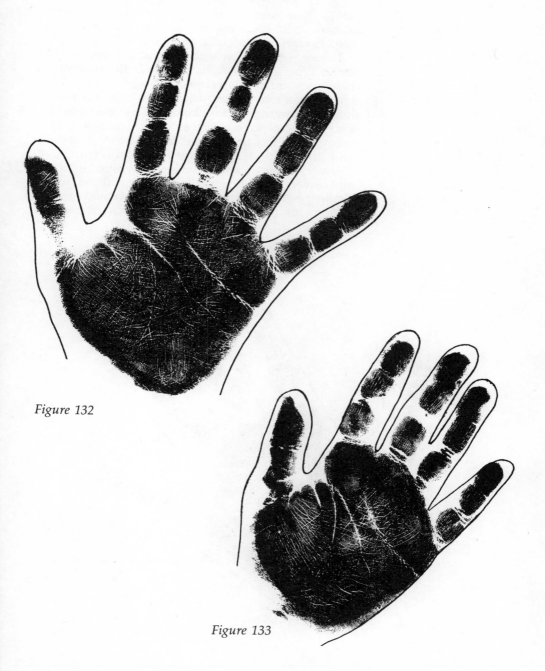

Figure 132

Figure 133

keeps them happy and stimulated. They are usually at their best studying the arts or humanities and project work is especially favoured.

Those with the spatulate-shaped palm are the active types. If the width is seen at the base of the hand they are likely to enjoy and excel in sports of all kinds. Don't try to coop up these children for too long indoors or in the classroom as their physical energies demand to be released in the playground or sports field. Restless mental energy belongs to those with the width at the top of the palm (Figure 134). These children need to explore, investigate, create and invent, so they will find any subject which challenges their minds to dig and delve and to work things out for themselves totally fascinating and exciting.

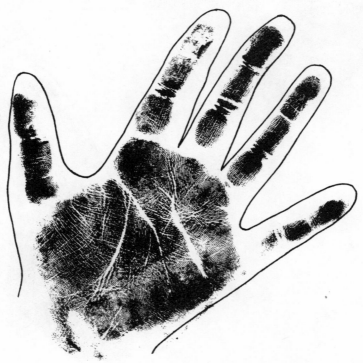

Figure 134

Figure 135

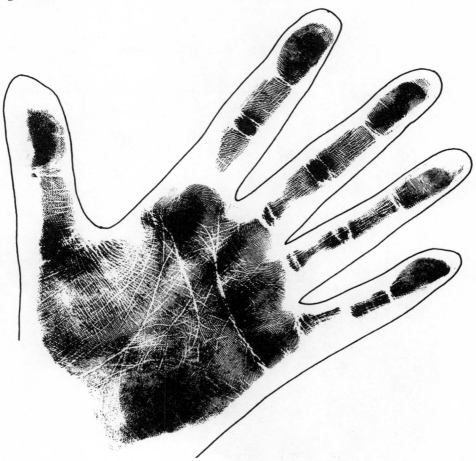

Long palms belong to children who prefer indoor pursuits (see Figure 135). They can become absorbed in detail so any close, intricate work would appeal to them. Often sensitive, idealistic and impressionable, they make good artists with a delicate sense of aesthetics. They can, at times, live entirely in their imagination, with their heads in the clouds, and so may suffer in a competitive environment. They may also find it difficult to cope with the nitty-gritty of everyday life.

FINGERS AND THUMBS

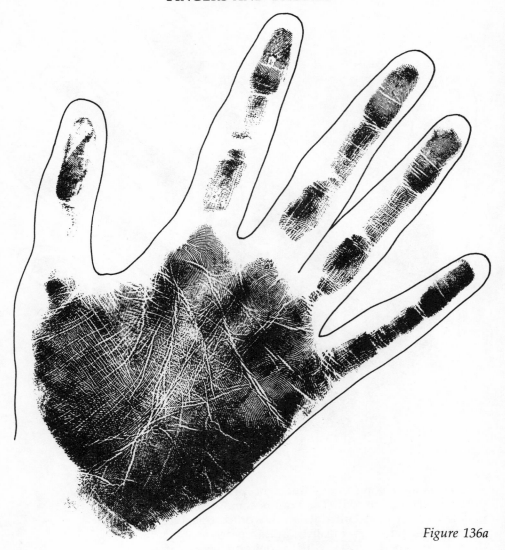

Figure 136a

It is the middle finger which is measured from tip to base in order to establish the length in comparison with the palm. When this digit is more than two-thirds the length of the palm, the fingers are said to be long but, if much less than this, then the fingers are considered short.

Long fingers denote an eye for detail and minutiae (Figure 136a). They suggest a careful and meticulous nature, one that is patient and thorough in every way.

Short fingers indicate quick, intuitive reactions (Figure 136b). These children can be impatient, especially with detail, and prefer to take an overall

Figure 136b

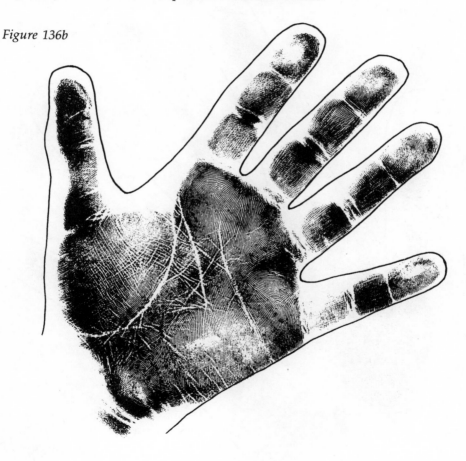

view rather than concentrate on the particular. They don't miss a trick for they learn quickly – albeit superficially at times – picking things up at a mere glance.

Fingers with marked protruding joints are called philosophical. These suggest a profound, analytical mind which, because it enjoys reflecting and pondering over ideas and problems, may be slow to respond. Smooth, pointed fingers, however, act on

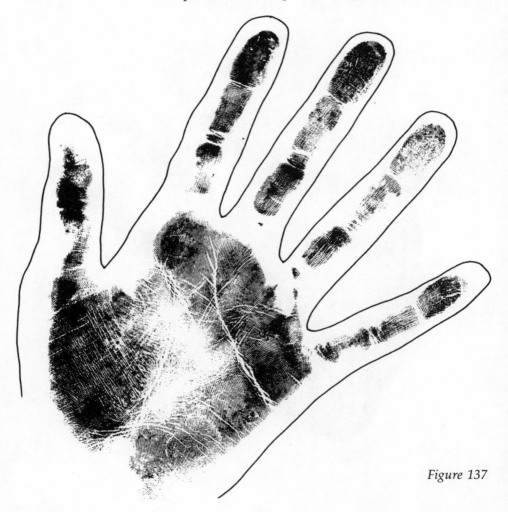

Figure 137

instinct where reactions and impressions seem to come and go with amazing speed, almost as if there were no time to process thought at all.

Two important points to look out for are connected with the index and little fingers. If the index is set very much lower down on the palm than the rest of the fingers it is an indication of a budding inferiority complex. When it is the little finger which is set too low, as in Figure 137, it suggests a fundamental lack of self-confidence. Children with these types of settings can be greatly helped to overcome their low self-esteem by giving them plenty of love together with masses of encouragement and support so they can believe in themselves and in their abilities. Without such positive direction their emotional and intellectual development could be blighted right through their adult lives.

When the hand is placed comfortably on the lap or on a table notice how the fingers are held. If the hand falls with the fingers more or less spread apart, the child will be open, generous, independent, excited with life, extroverted and generally happy-go-luckly. But when the fingers are held close together and the thumb falls at an acute angle then the child is likely to be introverted, possibly shy – the clingy, dependent type. If the fingers fall such that only the second and third are held together this shows a need for security and a harmonious family life. But when these two fingers are noticeably held apart it tells of a child who may be a bit of a loner, preferring solitary pursuits to the company of others.

The thumb represents reason and strength of will and should always look well proportioned, not overshadowed by the rest of the hand nor indeed dominating it. If the thumb does appear weak it highlights a child who is easily led, often swayed by stronger influences and who will go with the flow just for an easy life. If it looks out of balance because of its largeness the thumb tells of a strong character, one who can be forceful and dominant, perhaps sometimes even a bully. A well-balanced disposition, where will-power is tempered by reason, is seen when the thumb is a nice counterbalance to the rest.

THE LINES

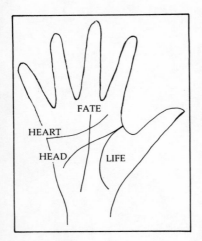

Figure 138

The life line (Figure 138) represents the physical quality of life and tells of enthusiasm for living. When the line is strong it denotes good physical strength and when chained, fragmented and islanded it suggests delicate health or physiological weakness. The closer to the thumb the line lies, the more reserved the child, the cooler the emotions and the lower the energy level. When the line sweeps further towards the centre of the palm, the child is more robust, recovers quickly after ill health and has plenty of energy and vitality. This shows a warm, outgoing and friendly disposition.

The head line highlights the mental or intellectual processes. Those children whose head lines begin widely separated from the life line are adventurous, sometimes to the point of foolhardiness. They are little daredevils, showing their independence from the word go. From then on they are impetuous and impulsive, constantly jumping in at the deep end with no thought of the consequences. A head line slightly detached, or even attached to the life line for a short way, tells of a sensible, confident attitude in life. But if, as in Figure 139, the two lines continue attached for a longer distance, it indicates dependence and over-cautiousness so that intellectually the child matures a little later than average and may be called a late-developer.

If the head line lies straight across the palm it illustrates a practical, pragmatic mind. Such children do best in scientific, mathematical, technological or purely practical subjects. If the line is curved then the imagination is rich and the inclination is more towards artistic or creative subjects. When it is at first straight and then curved there could be some confusion as to which camp to follow and perhaps one answer to this might be to think about a combination of the two, leading to subjects like the social sciences, geography, geology or history, for example.

A break in the line with a new section overlapping it, as illustrated in Figure 140, denotes a complete change of awareness and a new intellectual stance at the time indicated in the hand. This particular

Figure 139

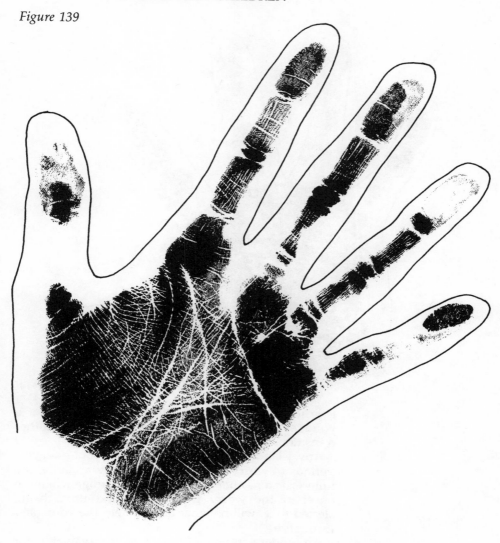

example shows that the change occurs around the late twenties. Before this time the child is likely to be practical, solid and down-to-earth but afterwards she is likely to find her wings, to become much more artistic, imaginative, and intellectual. Armed with this prior information, then, the parents might be

Figure 140

able to give her more creative encouragement at a younger age and thus prepare her for a smoother transition later on in her life.

Any islands seen on the head line could suggest periods of worry, anxiety or stress. By applying the time scale a mother would be able to judge when the onset of the worry is indicated and then, being alerted to it, will be more able to help the youngster through it.

An understanding of this line is invaluable for every parent as it clearly highlights a child's intellectual development and is critical when it comes to any advice on academic and career guidance. This particularly becomes relevant at that delicate time when children, at the tender age of thirteen or fourteen, have to choose the options which will then demarcate the course of the rest of their lives.

The fate line

Continuing with the theme of career and lifestyle, looking at the fate line will supply yet more information about these areas and will also reveal when possible changes are to be expected. A strong solid line which is unbroken from the wrist to the fingers is, these days, a rarity for it tells of the sort of life which is mapped out for the individual from birth to death. In the days when a son would follow in his father's footsteps, or a daughter's future of marriage and motherhood was a foregone conclusion, this would have been the line that described such fixed ways of life. But nowadays when youngsters can choose the type of occupation they would like to do and then change jobs or move or take up new careers at any time in their lives, the line is more than likely to show breaks, to alter course, throw up offshoots, etc.

If a youngster possesses a fate line which is very fragmented during its early part it denotes restlessness and a lack of direction in life (Figure 141a). Such a person would go from one job to another, doing this or that in the hope of eventually finding his or her niche. When the line strengthens into one solid groove then a true sense of direction has been found together with a career or style of life which brings security and stability (Figure 141b).

Any slight change of course or break seen in the line directly indicates a change within the occupational or domestic areas. If the change of direction is small then it implies merely a modification to the existing employment – new responsibilities, perhaps, or a promotion within the same firm. But if a break is seen where the new overlapping section begins at some distance away from the old one, it suggests a major change perhaps something like beginning a new job or career which might even entail moving house from one part of the country to another. By measuring this line it is possible to anticipate such changes and to be alerted to opportunities around that time. A mother, aware of these indications in the hands of her son or daughter could do much to help with interview techniques, for instance, or simply supply plenty of encouragement and moral support around those times.

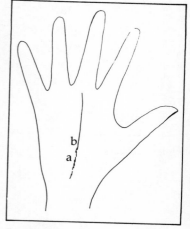

Figure 141

The heart line

The heart line will reveal much about a child's emotional attitude and how he or she will cope with relationships in life. Those whose lines begin high up between the first two fingers will be warm and loving with a tendency to show their feelings through little actions and deeds. The difficulty with these children is that they find it hard to actually talk about their inner emotions which often results in bottling up their feelings. Such children should be encouraged to express their passions verbally from a young age thus avoiding the possibility of repression in later life.

A line which begins towards the centre of the base of the index finger indicates a high achiever (Figure 142). Children with this marking will have extremely high standards and, unless helped to soften their attitudes or to make allowances for others, may find that people simply never come up to their expectations in life.

A line beginning lower down on the index mount tells of a romantic. These children are not very realistic about emotions, living in a rather rosy, fairy-tale world of relationships. They may be soft and dreamy children who would benefit from positive advice on the realities of life.

Children with the Simian line are very intense in everything they do and equally intense in their feelings. They can be extremely jealous when young, perhaps not mellowing until they have passed their mid-thirties.

Figure 142

Thus it can be seen what a wealth of information a mother can glean from the hand of her child. From it she can assess character and temperament, disposition and inclination, strengths and weaknesses, likes and dislikes. Empowered with such information she is in a better position to give guidance and advice from the very beginning of a child's life, not to interfere, but to encourage the child gently and to provide the sort of environment and background which will help that child to blossom and develop to the very best of his or her potential.

Chapter 8

FROM PUBERTY TO THE MENOPAUSE

Much reseach needs to be carried out on the effects of hormonal changes on the human hand. This is particularly relevant to women because of the major physical changes their bodies undergo at different stages in their lives. Not only do these changes occur at important developmental times such as puberty, pregnancy and the menopause, they happen at the much more regular intervals of the monthly menstrual cycle too. There are, of course, women who seem to sail right through these milestones with relatively little discomfort but others experience nothing but problems and complications throughout.

It is believed that particular glands belonging to the endocrine system are represented on the fingertips. The pituitary gland is reflected on the tip of the index finger, the pineal gland on the second, the thymus on the third and the thyroid on the little finger. Because the function of the pituitary is instrumental in menstruation, special attention will be paid to the index finger when considering the whole issue of the female reproductive cycle.

It must be remembered that this study requires much more extensive evidence before it can firmly establish that a relationship does indeed exist between the activity of the glands which are responsible for controlling the reproductive system, and their consequent markings on the fingertips. As yet, no direct correlation has been detected between the hand and the two important hormones, oestrogen and progesterone, which play such a major part in the whole process. Nevertheless, I put forward the theory that a connection does exist and, by concentrating on the pituitary and the index finger, I should like to stimulate interest in this area and hope that future research will put this theory to more stringent tests.

Figure 143a

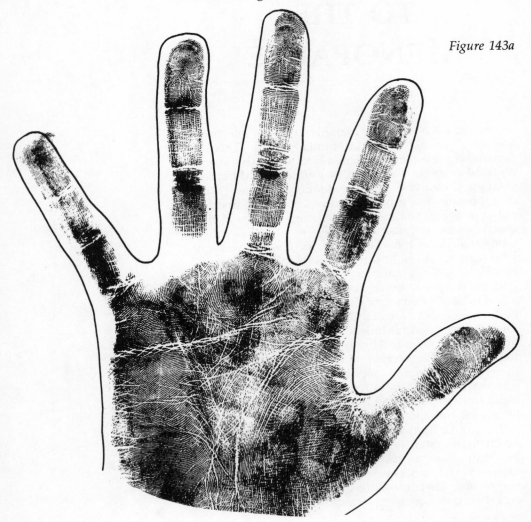

PUBERTY

The average age of puberty when the onset of menstruation occurs is usually, in the Western world, somewhere between 12 and 15 years. The physiological changes that take place in the transformation of child into young woman is quite dramatic. Enlargement of the breasts, growth of pubic hair and the filling out of hips, thighs and buttocks are all part

Figure 143b

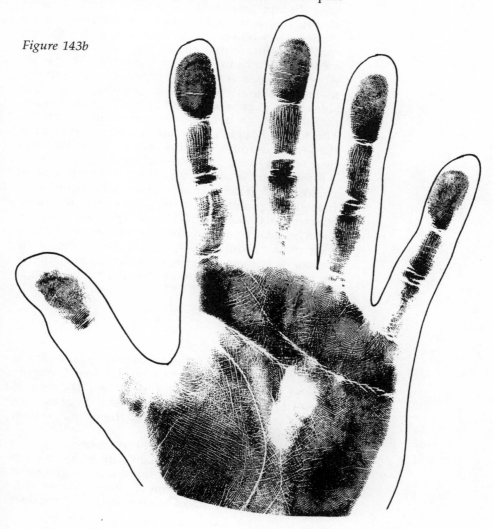

of the visible external changes that take place during this time of development, whilst internally, messages are being flashed from the hypothalamus and pituitary glands to release the hormones which will trigger the ovaries into action.

Figure 143a is the print of a 13-year-old girl who is showing all the external physical signs of reaching maturity although she has not yet started menstruating. The existence of both vertical and horizontal lines on her fingertips are evident, thus showing glandular activity, and especially prominent are those on her index finger which, according to the theory, would confirm that she is on the very threshold of menstruation. Figure 143b is the print of a 14-year-old who began menstruating for the first time about five months previously and it is interesting to note that she too has similar signs on her fingertips and again, that the lines on her index are especially noticeable. This hand, though, is not quite as strongly marked as the former example perhaps because her system has now settled into its natural rhythm.

If the theory is correct then this sort of information could be of great help to women who suffer with menstrual problems or who are plagued with premenstrual tension. It might be interesting for them to take a print of their hands say once every fortnight for about 4 to 6 months and try to detect any variations in the signs of any similar stress markings on their fingertips before menstruation and again at the time of ovulation.

PREGNANCY

Whilst menstruation is the monthly shedding of the lining of the uterus, ovulation (which occurs roughly around mid-cycle) is the time when the egg is released ready for fertilization. When the egg meets a sperm conception takes place and the woman is then effectively pregnant.

With pregnancy, as in puberty and menstruation, it is interesting to study the hand prints in order to detect any similar signs of hormonal or glandular activity. Figure 144 is the print of a lady taken roughly around the fifth month of her pregnancy. There does

Figure 144

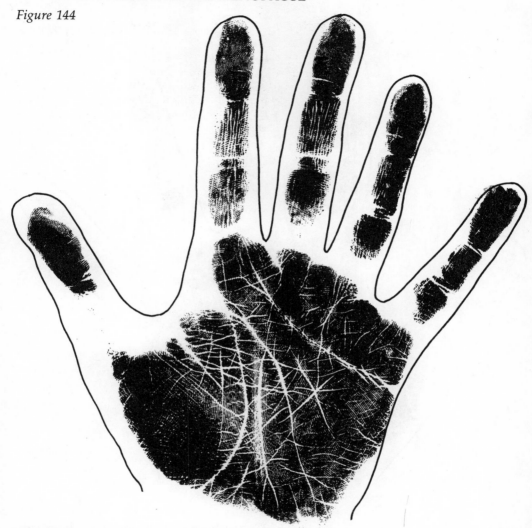

not seem to be much activity present on the index finger except for some very interesting white spots which were not the product of an injury, nor of a badly taken print.

Figure 145a is an example of the print of another pregnant lady, taken about two weeks after conception. Notice here the veiling, or criss-cross lines, on the tip of the index finger. Figure 145b was

Figure 145a

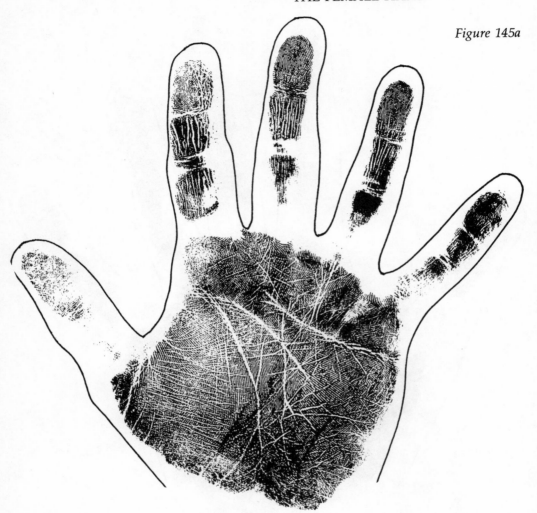

taken about two years later and the differences
between the two are most interesting. Here, there are
generally more lines all over the hand which would
confirm her busy and possibly even stressful life now
she has a young toddler to cope with. But, what is so
fascinating in this print is that despite the overall
increase of lines there is a definite *decrease* in the
veiling of the index finger!

This particular example shows that the signs of

Figure 145b

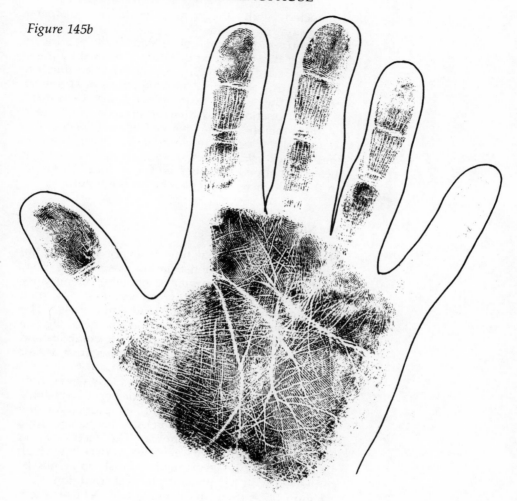

conception seem to be registered on the hand from the very beginning and it would be most interesting to follow up the study in order to determine how long it takes for the patterns to return to normal. This might indicate the length of time required, in each individual, for the return of her hormone balance to that prior to conception. Perhaps if more were known about the effects of hormone levels on the hand we might be better able to understand certain syndromes connected with pregnancy, such as postnatal depression for instance.

Of course, no firm conclusions can be drawn regarding this theory (and certainly not with a mere sample or two!). It is highly possible that the lines on the fingertips are simply showing signs of stress, or perhaps they may even correspond to totally different functions and their occurrence in all these hands is merely a coincidence. But nevertheless the coincidence *does* occur and it is fascinating to speculate on *why* it does. And such observations as these, it is hoped, may indeed focus future attention on the influences of pregnancy on the hand.

MENOPAUSE

The menopause is that time in every woman's life when ovulation and menstruation cease. In the West, the average age for a woman reaching the menopause is around fifty although it can occur at any time between the early forties and mid-fifties. The menopause is often known as 'the change of life' – a change which may take several years to complete and which may involve different symptoms such as, for instance, the notorious hot flushes.

Figure 146 is a print belonging to a lady who is now going through the menopause. For her it has been a difficult time with unpleasant symptoms ranging from dizzy spells, anxiety attacks, anaemia and, for a short time, even agoraphobia. The fact that her fingertips are covered in lines reflect the high glandular activity levels which must no doubt be connected with her present physical condition.

Figure 147 is the print of a lady who believes she is now coming to the end of the change of life. It has been a process which for her has taken seven to eight years to complete and has had unpleasant symptoms such as depression, hot flushes and migraine – so much so that she was forced to give up her job altogether. Now that she is almost over the menopause, however, her fingertips are showing fewer lines than the former example but, in comparison to the second and third fingers, the index tip seems to be remarkably clear.

Again, further research needs to be carried out here too in order to establish the relationship between the menopause and the consequent hormonal activity that is registered on the hand.

Figure 146

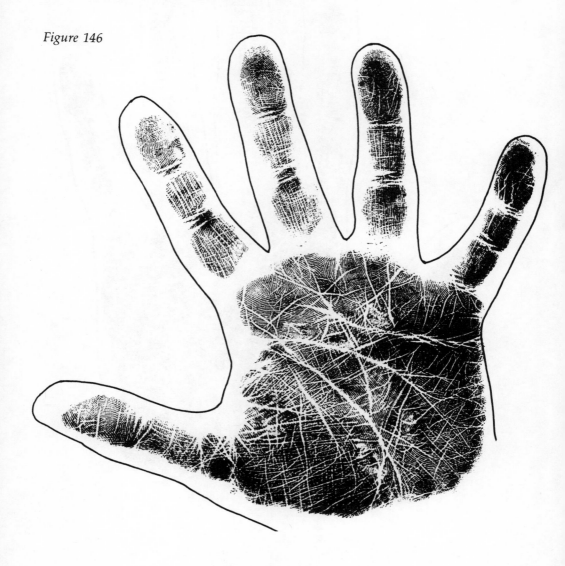

Figure 147

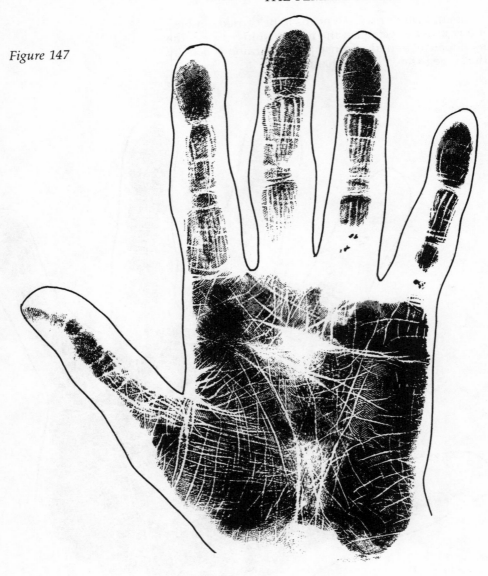

Chapter 9
FAMILY HEALTH

The hand is a wonderful reflector of the physical and psychological health of the individual. First and foremost it is a mirror of the individual's *predisposition* to ill health – which does not mean that the indications marked on the hand will inevitably develop into full-blown clinical disease. And secondly, it can act as an early-warning system of the likelihood of future ill health.

Studying the health patterns depicted on the hand is not an exercise for the anxious, highly imaginative type and certainly not recommended for the hypochondriac, as the effect can be the same at that of leafing through a medical encyclopaedia only to finish up thinking that you have every symptom described in the book! However, an assessment of the possible weak links in the individual's mental and physiological make-up can be an important and valuable application of hand analysis.

For a woman, particularly, this can be a most useful exercise because, by knowing what to look for, she can detect the indications of ill health on the hands of those close to her and then keep a watchful eye on any signs of development. But in analysing the hand for these indications she must, above all, be circumspect, that is, she must take everything into account before making any final judgements – no single factor can stand alone but must be refined and modified, confirmed and corroborated by all others in order for a true picture to emerge. Equally, it is dangerous to diagnose from the hand alone and this must be left to the qualified medical practitioner. So, if any real doubts or worries should occur when analysing a hand it is always wisest to consult one's family doctor rather than labour under any anxieties or misconceptions.

There are several areas in the hand which reflect aspects of health. The colour and temperature of the hand are the first indications to consider and sometimes the shape, too, can reveal the psychological attitude to the whole question of health and disease. More information then lies in the nails, the skin patterns and in the lines themselves.

Before attempting any analysis it must be stressed again that any findings may simply reveal the individual's inherited predisposition to particular conditions. Indeed, most people have natural weaknesses; some are prone to circulatory disorders, some to gynaecological complaints, others to pulmonary problems and so on. But, because they have these weak links, it does not follow that disease will necessarily manifest itself. And even if this were likely, the beauty of hand analysis as an early-warning system is that it gives the individual plenty of time to take preventive measures or at least to deal with the problem before it develops into a chronic pathological disorder. Remember, too, that lines on the hand can change and that if any indications of adverse health are detected and dealt with in time they can repair themselves and disappear altogether.

There are many factors which reveal how the individual copes with the whole question of health and the first lies in the structure of the hand itself. The more solid the hand looks, the stronger the constitution – a thin, frail looking hand would suggest a certain physiological delicacy.

If the mount of Venus is large and full so that the life line encircling it sweeps well out into the centre of the palm, it will reveal a person who is blessed with robust health, plenty of energy and vitality and a goodly supply of sound physical resources (Figure 148a). This individual is the sort who will shake off any illness and who seems able to recuperate and

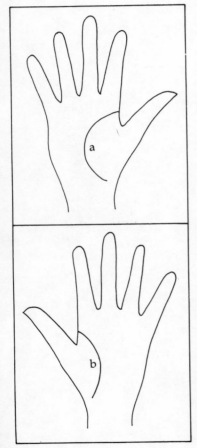

Figure 148

bounce back after any period of ill health. But a thin, narrow mount of Venus, one where the life line hugs itself tightly around the thumb, shows a susceptibility to disease for this person does not have an abundance of energy, is considered a physically weak type with a delicate constitution and is thus prone to ill health and has a tendency to catch anything that's 'going round' (Figure 148b).

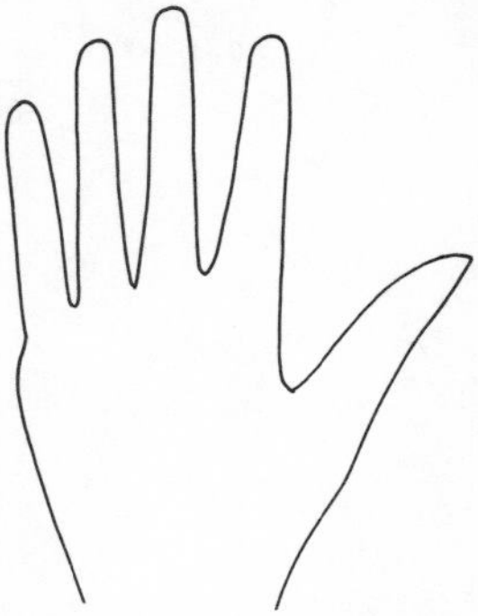

Figure 150

Figure 149

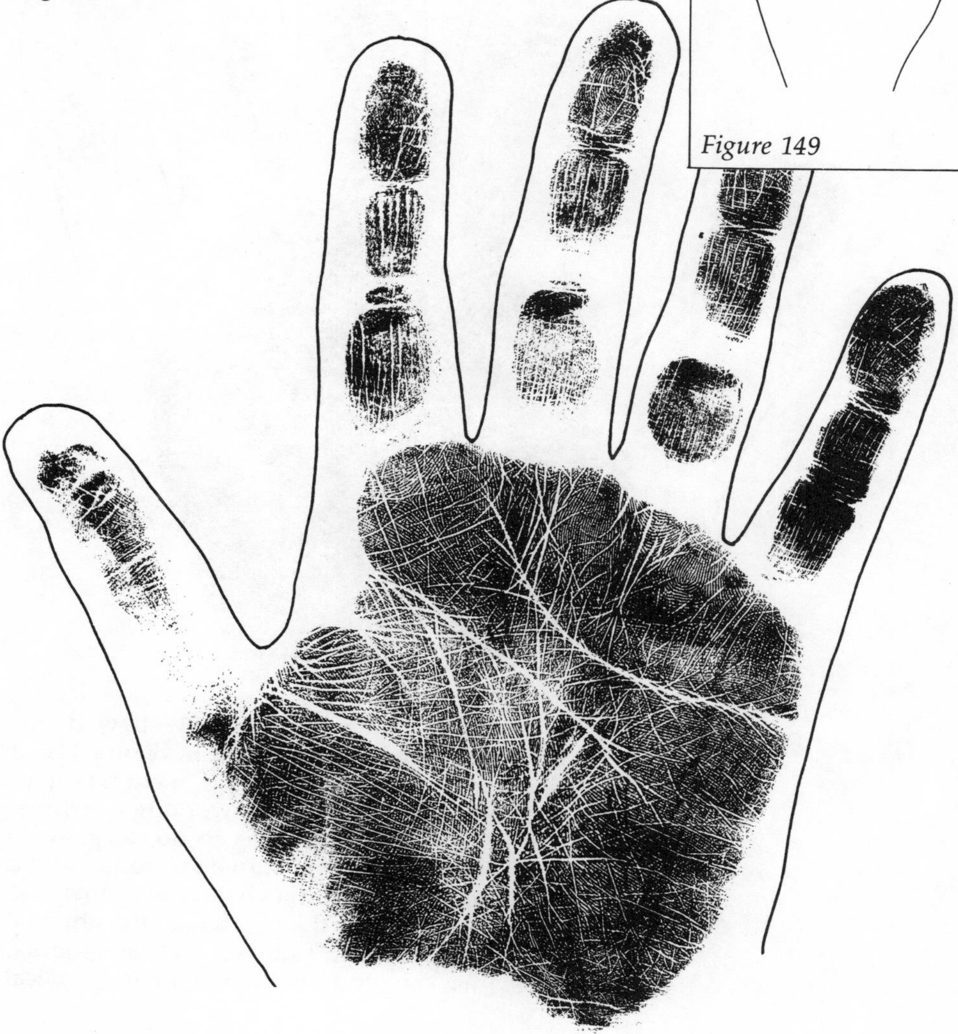

Figure 151

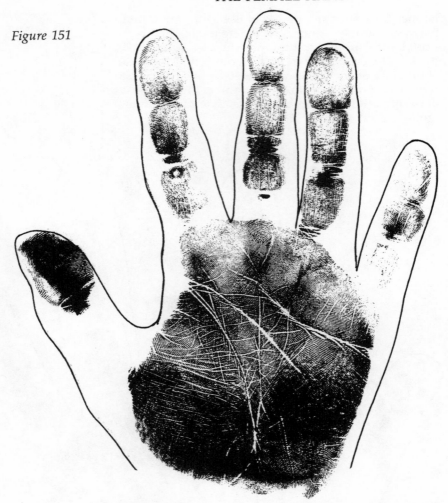

If the percussion edge is noticeably bowed just below the little finger, as illustrated in Figure 149, it reveals a person who is what I call a 'mental fidget', that is, whose mind is constantly working overtime, always thinking of the next thing to do, to plan, to consider. These restless minds drive the bodies and if the base of their palms are much narrower than the tops it shows that they do not have the physical resources to keep up the pace set by their minds. Sometimes this can end up in complete physical exhaustion so people with this type of hand should make sure they get plenty of rest – some yoga or deep breathing relaxation exercises wouldn't go amiss either.

There is an important distinction between those with the 'full' and those with the 'empty' hand when it comes to health. A full hand, as in Figure 150, is one where the palm seems to be covered in many fine lines rather like a spider's web, whilst the empty hand, shown in Figure 151, contains just the major lines with very few incidental ones so that it presents a most uncomplicated picture. The more lines there are in the palm, the more complex the personality is likely to be. Such a person might be considered a highly-strung, anxious type with a great degree of sensitivity to her nervous system which makes her more aware of any pain or discomfort in her body. Although not insensitive, the lady with the 'empty' hand, however, is much calmer, appears to be far less troubled by her constitution and consequently is the sort who is very rarely ill, never seems to miss a day's work and if she does happen to have the misfortune to be ill, simply manages to rise above it or makes a dramatic recovery and continues on where lesser mortals would be laid up for at least a fortnight!

The colour and temperature of the hand are also important indicators of the state of health but care should be taken to check these when the individual is at rest and not immediately after strenuous exercise. Also the temperature of the hand should be compared to the prevailing weather conditions so that a hand blue with cold on a frosty January morning is not mistakenly interpreted as indicative of a sluggish circulation. However, if the hand (and indeed all the extremities) is normally cold, perhaps even with a hint of blueness, this could be pointing to circulatory problems.

On the contrary, a red hand which is usually hot shows a predisposition to feverish conditions. If the hands are not only red and hot but also dry and rough they may be an indication of an under-active thyroid. When they are not dry but constantly clammy they could be denoting an over-active thyroid although this is also seen on those who are prone to allergic reactions. When a European hand,

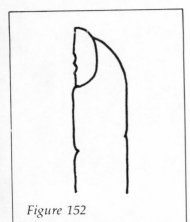

Figure 152

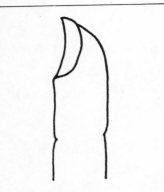

Figure 153

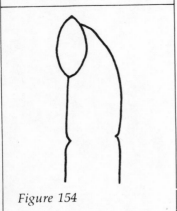

Figure 154

which does not normally have an olive or sallow complexion, shows marked signs of yellowness it may indicate problems of the liver such as jaundice, biliousness or perhaps hepatitis. A very white skin on the hand, unless on someone with a pale complexion, may point to anaemia.

The fingernails, too, are splendid indicators of health and much information is contained in both their colour and construction. At their best, again on the European hand, they should be a light pink in colour with a neat, milky-white half-moon, and gently curved from cuticle to tip. Just as with the hand, the colour of the nails is important to note. A decidedly bluish tinge to the nail can suggest poor circulation but also may hint at weaknesses of the heart or lungs. Further information can be seen in the appearance of the half-moon – an inordinately large one may point to potential cardiac disorders whilst non-existent moons highlight possible pulmonary trouble. When the nail is very white it tells of an anaemic condition and thus a lack of iron, whereas too much iron may be indicated in the bright red nail which also denotes a hot-blooded, fiery temperament and consequently all the associated illnesses that go with this kind of disposition.

White specks in the nail have long been known to indicate a calcium inbalance but there are other features which also highlight mineral deficiencies. A large cuticle often denotes such a condition but so too do tiny dents and horizontal ridges in the nail. (Figure 152). These latter formations are most interesting for, when seen, they invariably denote that something has gone wrong with the diet and, as the nail takes approximately six months to grow from its base to the top of the quick, it is possible to determine when the individual's diet went awry. For example, a horizontal groove half-way up the nail would indicate that the problem occurred about three months previously, further up might suggest about five months previously and at the base, it tells that the present diet is lacking some of the essential vitamins or minerals necessary for a balanced diet and good health.

Nails that break or flake easily or those which are markedly dished, as in Figure 153, also represent poor nutrition whilst very convexed ones, like that shown in Figure 154, are known as 'Hippocratic nails' and as such highlight pulmonary weaknesses or disorders. It is recommended that smokers who possess the Hippocratic nail should strongly consider giving up the habit. Vertical ridging, however, is quite different and often suggests allergic sensitivities (Figure 155).

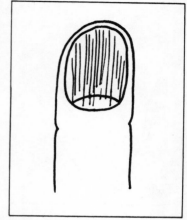

Figure 155

An important point to be made here is that, because many of these signs have alternative meanings, all the indications concerning health must be corroborated by other features in the hand before any final conclusions are drawn. It has already been said, for example, that the temperature of the hand must be interpreted according to the prevailing ambience and taking into account any recent physical activity. Equally so, care should be taken when assessing a horizontal ridge on the nail, for instance, because whilst it can denote poor nutrition it may, under certain circumstances, also represent a shock or an accident that occurred at that particular time in the subject's life, and this case would be confirmed by, perhaps, a trauma line across the life line.

The study of the fingerprints and skin ridges (dermatoglyphics) for medical purposes is still in its early stages but already much interesting information is emerging. The skin patterns are formed in the early months of foetal development and particular patterns, it has been discovered, represent specific congenital malformations or chromosomal abnormalities.

It has been established that skin patterns are inherited so that where there are any congenital abnormalities, as these are passed on so too are the accompanying dermatoglyphics. For this reason the study of dermatoglyphics has an important place as an aid to genetic counselling. Also, when any mishap occurs during those first few crucial months of embryonic life – let's say if a pregnant mother contracts German measles – the resultant abnormality is reflected in the very skin ridges of the new-born child.

On a healthy hand the actual skin ridges should be clear and unbroken and although, unlike the lines, the skin patterns we are born with never change they

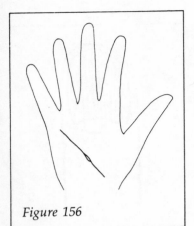

Figure 156

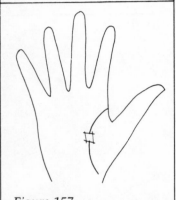

Figure 157

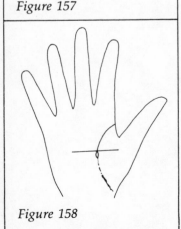

Figure 158

can under certain conditions start to show signs of breaking up. When this occurs it can reveal that the system is out of order and therefore the individual is more disposed to the onset of disease. With care and attention, proper rest, nutrition and exercise, the ridges can rebuilt themselves and thus predict recovery and regained health.

The quality and construction of the lines are further indicators of the state of the individual's health. At their best, lines should be clearly marked without any islands, chains, breaks or cross-bars to impede their flow. When they do occur most of these indications can be timed and dated by using the timing gauges described in Chapters 4 and 5.

Islands occurring in the head line suggest periods of worry and anxiety. In the heart, life and hepatica (see Figure 156) lines, islands point to a certain predisposition to disease, and they may also denote actual periods of ill health and constitutional weakness when they appear on the life line. Chains on most of the major lines may suggest mineral imbalances.

Clean breaks in the lines need to be thoroughly investigated for they can indicate sudden accidents or a serious bout of ill health. Interestingly, if the break is covered by a set of four tiny lines in the formation of a square it denotes that circumstances surrounding the event will either moderate the gravity of the situation or afford some sort of protection to the individual (Figure 157). Either way, a complete recovery may well be hoped for when this particular configuration is present.

Cross-bars, which here include trauma lines, always show emotional upsets, opposition to or interference with the subject's normal course of life and as such obviously debilitate the system.

Always note the condition of the line after whatever impediment is seen as this will tell how the individual will cope with the adversity implied. If the line returns to normal then recovery will ensue but if the construction of the line is weakened after the event, as illustrated in Figure 158, then the health may be impaired as a result. Yet again, remember that such indications of ill health, if detected and dealt with in time, can disappear or at least give the individual plenty of time to avert the situation altogether.

THE HEAD

Obviously, in any condition affecting the head it is on the head line itself that most attention will be focused. Headaches, and more usually migraine, may be detected here by a series of tiny indentations, or sometimes white spots, which are clearly visible when the line is stretched (Figure 159a). Any fuzziness of the line can indicate a form of dizziness or certainly an inability to concentrate which can lead to difficulty in making clear decisions (Figure 159b).

Islands here do show worries and these may contribute to a weakening of the general constitution (Figure 160a). When a dip is seen in the line, and especially if a tiny branch shoots down from it, this can be an indication of depression (Figure 160b).

A clean break in the line as in Figure 160c, where the two ends are not overlapped can show a sudden injury to the head – an accident, a fall or a blow – and in this case other areas of the hand should be analysed, particularly the life line, which will give further information about this situation.

EYES, EARS AND TEETH

Any indications concerning the eyes, ears or teeth are usually seen on or above the heart line. An island in this line directly beneath the ring finger often points to problems with the sight (Figure 161a). This formation is usually seen on those who may need to wear spectacles.

Another island in the heart line, but this time beneath the middle finger, invariably suggests hearing impairment (Figure 161b).

Teeth and gum disorders may be detected by tiny vertical or oblique lines which lie just above the heart line beneath the little finger (Figure 161c). These should not be confused with the medical stigmata which occurs in the same area but which is a much larger configuration of lines.

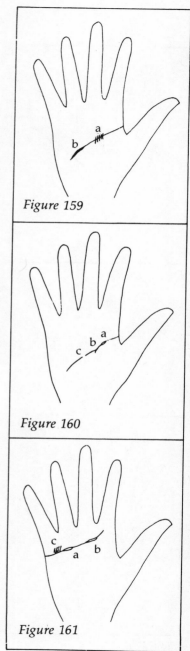

Figure 159

Figure 160

Figure 161

THE LUNGS

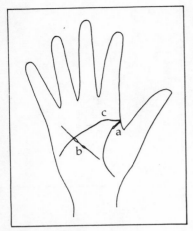

Figure 162

Various areas in the hand are associated with the respiratory tract. The colour and formation of the nails provide several clues here. Although a bluish tinge is more commonly indicative of circulatory problems it might in some cases also allude to bronchial or pulmonary trouble too. The Hippocratic nail is one which is markedly humped and this is a long established indicator of weaknesses or disorders of the respiratory system. Nails which curve around the fingertips can indicate poor oxygenation and may be found amongst heavy smokers or those who have recently given up the habit.

Islands at the very beginning of the life line denote childhood illnesses and more often than not also suggest pulmonary weaknesses and susceptibility to any respiratory problems (Figure 162a). This may also be confirmed by islands occurring in the hepatica or Mercury line (Figure 162b).

The throat too may come under this category and when the head line arches upwards as it travels beneath the gap between the first and second fingers, it can imply a tendency to all manner of throat infections, especially so if an island is present here too (Figure 162c). Occasionally, when this formation is seen in conjunction with poorly shaped nails it can point to a tendency towards an asthmatic condition.

THE HEART AND CIRCULATION

Figure 163

The colour of the hands and the nails provide the first clues to the cardio-vascular system and further information is contained within the heart line itself. Very red hands or those which are cold and bluish in colour are often indications of circulatory problems. The same applies to the nails, especially so if the base has a marked blue tinge to it and both the very red and the blue nail suggest cardiac weaknesses.

A chained heart line, which can denote mineral imbalances, can also suggest irregularities in the action of the heart (Figure 163a), whereas one long island in the line towards the percussion edge may point, it has been said, to a predisposition to high blood-pressure (Figure 163b). A complete break in the line as illustrated in Figure 163c, although rare, has been noticed in some cases of cardiac arrest but this, as well as all other indications, needs further investigation and should be accepted as a theory rather than a proven fact.

THE LIVER

On the average European hand, any yellowing of the skin which is clearly not part of a tan or of a sallow complexion is associated with liver dysfunction. This also applies to the nails where they may show an overall yellow tinge or isolated yellow spots or patches.

THE SKELETON

Broken bones may occur in sudden accidents and when these are serious they may be represented by a break in a line, an island or crossing trauma line. A fine line rising upwards from the life line in the direction of the middle finger can often denote a broken bone, especially so if the line rises from the very point where another of the indications, such as a crossing bar, occurs. Figure 164 illustrates this sort of example.

The spinal column is also associated with the life line and an island situated about one-third of the way down, roughly where the line passes beneath the middle finger, can denote a predisposition to back trouble (Figure 165).

THE REPRODUCTIVE SYSTEM

The area corresponding to the reproductive system is located at the very base of the palm, just above the wrist, on the percussion side of the hand. If the skin ridge patterns here become broken up, or if this part is heavily lined, it suggests disorders of the reproductive organs (Figure 166a). When the top rascette arches up into the palm itself it can denote

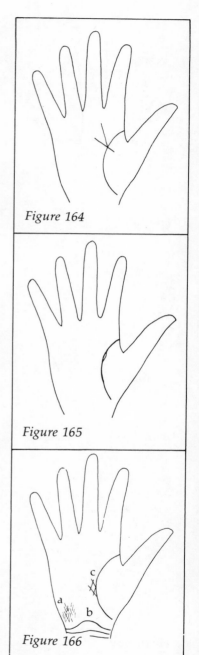

Figure 164

Figure 165

Figure 166

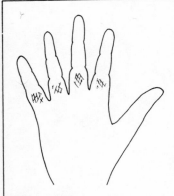

Figure 167

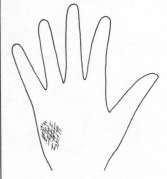

Figure 168

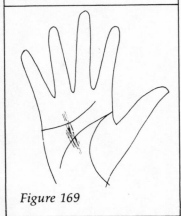

Figure 169

internal delicacy and may indicate difficulties or complications in childbirth (Figure 166b).

A diamond or triangular formation of lines occurring about a third of the way up the palm and attached to the outside of the life line can also imply a susceptibility to problems of the reproductive organs, whether it be irregularities of the menstrual cycle or organic disorders (Figure 166c). Regular checks are recommended for women who posses this configuration because, although not an absolute proof of the likelihood of disease in this area, it could nevertheless be an early warning sign.

Otherwise, this pattern can suggest a predisposition to problems of the lower intestines, whilst on a man's hand this same formation can point to urogenital problems and in some cases it has been associated with those suffering with a hernia.

THE DIGESTIVE TRACT

The digestive tract, as represented on the hand, is interesting because, as it is a complex function, indications pertaining to it are scattered all over the place.

The teeth and gums which obviously have their own part to play have already been discussed (page 185). Any dental problems can be seen as tiny lines above the heart line and beneath the little finger but these can also be the first clues to stomach or liver trouble. With liver dysfunction the yellowing of the skin and nails would be a corroborating factor. Large and full basal phalanges on the index fingers which are heavily criss-crossed with lines might also call the stomach into question (Figure 167).

A build-up of acidity (thus including the renal and urinary system) or further stomach or intestinal disorders may be observed by the breakdown of the skin ridges on the palm. If the impairment of the ridges is seen towards the percussion edge, in that area between the head and heart lines as depicted in Figure 168, it shows that the acidity levels could reach such proportions as to lead to rheumatic conditions. Careful diet and nutrition can correct the condition if dealt with in time.

If heavy lining or a breakdown of the ridges occurs in the band of the palm directly beneath the ring finger, from the middle of the fate line and rising up towards the heart line, it is indicative of gastric or intestinal complaints (Figure 169).

THE NERVOUS SYSTEM

A person who is nervous or highly-strung can be seen at a glance by the very shape of the hand. The longer, finer and more pointed the hand, the more nervy the disposition. When the percussion edge bows out markedly just below the little finger it tells of an over-active mentality, a fidgety mind which drives the body, often using up precious physical reserves and thus sometimes leading to nervous exhaustion. Mental relaxation exercises are highly recommended for these types. They are also recommended for anyone with a distinctly long, deeply bowed head line which sweeps down into the depths of the Luna mount. These people are so highly imaginative that they get quite carried away by the very force of their imagination. Such a head line suggests bouts of depression and melancholia when the heightened creativity of the individual is not positively channelled and directed.

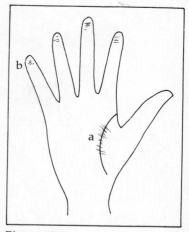

Figure 170

A 'full hand' is another example of a nervous disposition for it shows a particular sensitivity to one's nervous system. A series of fine lines, which might otherwise be mistaken for trauma lines, which cross the life line throughout its course, is another indication of the highly anxious person who has a tendency to over-worry (Figure 170a). Fine horizontal lines occurring on the fingertips may be another sign of stress and tension (Figure 170b). These can come and go over a remarkably short period of time according to the stresses and strains experienced in the individual's life.

Finally, quite often after serious accidents or major surgery several star formations may occur all over the hand. Stars such as these denote shock to the central nervous system and disappear again with the individual's recovery and improved health.

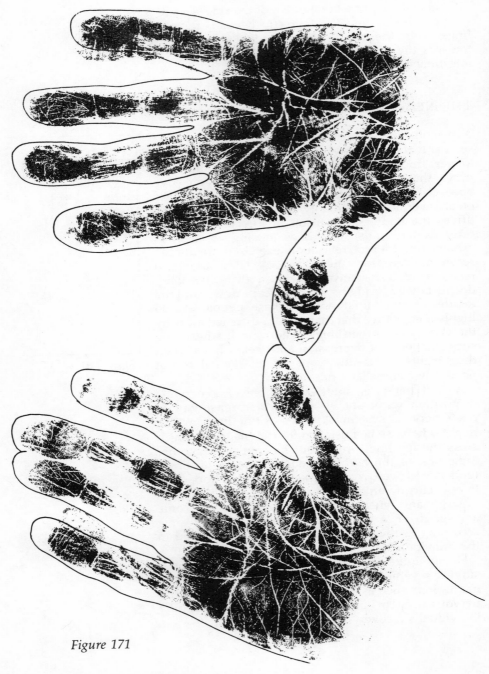

Figure 171

FAMILY HEALTH

A QUESTION OF LONGEVITY

Figure 171 comprises the hand prints of a lady who, having been born in 1882, has now reached the remarkable age of 103. Although heavily lined in places, it is still quite possible to see the major lines with clarity and ease. The head line is long, the life line is strong and the heart line is deep and clearly etched. The length of the head line, with its noticeable lack of islands, interference marks or fraying of any kind, testifies to the fact that she's still as bright as a button and, although she obviously tires easily, she is able to hold a considerably long and interesting conversation, remembering events quite clearly right back into her childhood.

Signs of glandular activity are evident on the fingertips; the Venus mount has, with age, lost some of its fullness and the veiling on the right percussion also confirms the arthritis she suffers in her hip and back. However, it cannot be denied that, for 103, these prints present a truly remarkable picture. When asked to what she attributes her long life she answered: a happy marriage, albeit with no children, a contented life and only just a drop of sherry now and then!

Chapter 10
KEEPING TABS

The recurrent message that runs right through this book is that, once we have learnt the basic principles, we can use hand analysis to monitor our progress through life – to keep tabs on what's going on. The quintessential fact to remember is that the hand can change, that we are not necessarily stuck with any of the indications, for these simply highlight the possibilities of future events and not, in every case, irrevocable absolutes. Moreover, the fact that we possess free will means that we have the power to make choices in our lives. Obviously, the choice for each individual is not unlimited but at least within our own sphere of influence we can make decisions and it is this very ability to choose that gives us personal power over our immediate environment.

So, by understanding the potential that is marked in our hands we can then decide whether to enhance and develop any of our innate talents or, if we consider them to be negative, we may choose to let them lie dormant or possibly even try to correct them. Similarly, when it comes to indications of future events, by learning to recognize our hands, we will become attuned to any tiny changes in the lines which act as an advanced warning and which we may then be able to intercept and act upon accordingly.

Just as we might have regular check-ups at the dentist, so it is of great benefit to look at our hands periodically in order to catch any subtle changes at the early stages of their formation. During this exercise, however, we should take care to avoid becoming introspective for this would make us too subjective and then our judgement becomes suspect. So we must try to stand aloof, to investigate the hand with as much objectivity as we can bring to the exercise. One way of distancing ourselves is to work from a print rather than from the hand itself. Moreover, taking prints of our own hands and those of our loved ones at regular intervals is also an excellent way of keeping a permanent record of each individual's growth and development. For this exercise a check-list may be drawn up which would contain the individual's personal characteristics, including inherent gifts and talents, together with the times of anticipated future events. Then, around every six or twelve months, say, a new print can be taken and the list can be checked for any development of the individual's potential, for corroboration with events that have actually taken place and updated with any further changes predicted for the future.

A regular assessment of hand prints in this way can be carried out for each member of the family, friends, or relatives within one's circle and an extremely valuable comparative analysis would be to trace any similarities in future indications between hands. Another interesting aspect is to evaluate the influence one person's actions or decisions have upon the lives of the others in the same circle.

For example, the fate line in a father's hand might show signs of a change of job which would involve moving to a new part of the country. His head line might, at that time, throw a new branch in the direction of the middle finger, whilst another branch from the fate line might shoot off towards the ring finger. All these indications suggest that the new job for him implies promotion, a real step forward in his career which will bring greater stability, financial rewards and more personal satisfaction.

The hands of his two young sons also show positive signs of growth and happiness. The move for them comes as an adventure and the trends in their head lines reveal an expansion of mind which may not have occurred without this broadening of their horizons.

The hand of his wife, however, tells quite a different story. For her, the upheaval of moving house with two young sons, having to leave an area in which she has lived for many years and where she has developed close, intimate friends in order to exchange all this for the uncertainty of a new life comes as a wrench and as such is represented by a series of strong trauma lines crossing her main life line. At the same time an island is seen on her head line which shows that the process of readjustment for her will not be at all easy and may even take considerable time.

This example demonstrates how the actions of one person can determine those of another and it is an exercise which can be applied to the prints of any interrelated group of people with very interesting results. But such an assessment is of far more value if used for forward planning as it can alert the individual to any likely forthcoming trends and appropriate action can then be taken accordingly. For instance, in the example above, had the members of that family recognized the indications in their hands, they would have seen the wife's discontented reactions to the proposed move and might have found some way in which to cushion her from the full force of the events and support her through the changes. They might, let's say, have discussed the implications of a new job for one, even two years beforehand so as to become gradually accustomed to the whole idea of change. Or, nearer to the move, they could have spent several weekends in the new location, familiarizing themselves with the area, possibly treating these holidays as romantic get-aways or as a second honeymoon, thus instilling a sense of fun into the whole venture. With time and the kind of advanced warning that is provided by the indications on the hand, much could have been done to make the most of the situation and to avoid any unnecessary distress.

Thus, when assessing the hand for future trends there are several signs to look out for and in particular these are the trauma lines, islands, breaks or changes in direction in the lines and also, of course, any branches too.

TRAUMA LINES

These are bold lines which cut across the life line and can start from any point on the mounts of Lower Mars or Venus, ending just across the line, or may continue to cut any of the other major lines of fate, head or heart. Whenever seen they represent upheavals of some kind, and more usually than not, emotional upsets. Some are stronger than others and it is the strength which registers the depth of feeling surrounding the events at the time.

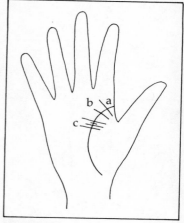

Figure 172

Trauma lines can be marked off against the life line, using the timing gauge described in Chapter 4, thus enabling events to be dated and put into context. If a truama line is seen crossing the life line high up at its beginning it is a sign of early childhood problems and anxieties (Figure 172a). Often several of these may occur during the turbulent adolescent years when youngsters are trying to cope with their bodily changes whilst at the same time getting to grips with their emotions or attempting to make bids for independence. Further along, a strong trauma line might indicate more emotional upheaval in connection with romantic involvements (Figure 172b). Parental interference or displeasure here can so often result in the presence of bold trauma lines, especially so if they begin on the family ring, and if these are seen in advance then the parents can be alerted to deal with their youngsters in a sensitive and understanding manner and to try to take the pressure off them.

On many hands a series of trauma lines may exist crossing the section of life line representing the twenties and thirties and these would suggest problems associated with the early responsibilities of life: making strides in one's career; worrying about relationships, marriage, partnerships, break-ups or divorce; adjusting to the birth and early development of children; coping with anxieties about ageing parents (Figure 172c). Lower down on the life line, any further traces of these crossing lines are interpreted in the same way as indications of emotional upheaval. The general rule throughout is that the deeper or longer the line, the stronger the upset. These trauma lines, however, must not be confused with the many fine lines which are seen in some hands across the whole length of the life line because these, rather than pointing to emotional upsets, merely represent a nervy, highly-strung individual.

ISLANDS

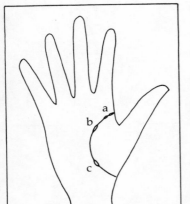

Figure 173

Islands are a negative sign whenever and wherever seen for they represent a split in the flow of the energy denoted by the line. On the life line they invariably indicate a lowering of resistance, a time when the life force is at a low ebb or they may simply denote ill health. Sometimes, though, rather than actual ill health they may just indicate a weakness or a predisposition to a particular disease which, with care, may never even develop into a clinical condition.

Islands at the very beginning of the life line can represent early childhood illnesses and in particular any troubles connected with the bronchial or respiratory tract (Figure 173a). Further down, lying where the line crosses beneath the middle finger, an island might suggest a predisposition to back or spinal problems (Figure 173b). Situated towards the end of the line, it can signify any of the illnesses related to old age (Figure 173c). In addition, at any point on the line, an island may register a physical injury such as one sustained in an accident or a car crash, for instance.

If the illness or injury is a traumatic one then the island could well be accompanied by a strong crossing line and sometimes, if there are any bones broken, a fine line may be pushed up, from the very point depicting the time when the injury took place, towards the middle finger (Figure 174). Inspecting the quality and structure of the life line for repair or weaknesses after the presence of the island will determine whether full recovery will be made (if the line is restored to its normal strength and vigour), or indeed, whether there will be any lasting detrimental effects due to the event (if the line shows any signs of degeneration).

When an island is seen on the head line it illustrates

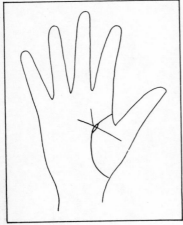

Figure 174

that the full flow of mental energy is not being channelled in one strong direction. This, then, invariably suggests worry or a time of indecision and self-doubt; a time, at least, when the thought processes are far from being at their best. Again, an analysis of the line before and after the island will reveal the sort of influence the event has had upon the individual's thinking.

An island on the fate line directly refers to anxieties associated with the individual's career or way of life. It may indicate that some dissatisfaction exists here, trouble at work or conflict with colleagues. In many instances on this line it may also reflect financial worries.

On the Sun line an island suggests unhappiness which lasts for the duration of the island itself. Traditionally, an island here has been interpreted as representing scandal which has a detrimental effect on the subject's reputation and good name.

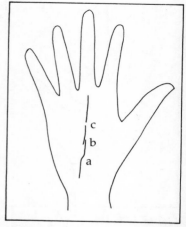

Figure 175

CHANGES OF DIRECTION AND BREAKS IN THE LINES

These two formations may be classified as either positive or negative markings depending on where they occur, the nature of their formation and how the individual is prepared to deal with the indications they represent.

Changes of direction are mainly associated with the fate line and when seen denote a change of either the individual's job or way of life (Figure 175a). Whereas the change of direction normally suggests different responsibilities or a side-step of some kind, a break in the line invariably represents a complete change, whether in the career or domestically. If the break in the line is overlapped by a new section, as in Figure 175b, it indicates that the subject has planned the change for herself but, if the line shows a clean break, illustrated in Figure 175c, then the change has been suddenly forced upon the individual from agents or circumstances outside of her control. The wider the break or the space between the overlap, the greater the change. Once again, an examination of the line after the interruption will instantly reveal whether it was for better or worse.

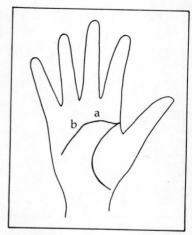

Figure 176

A change of direction is sometimes seen on the head line and here would suggest a change of attitude, perspective or awareness. If the head line suddenly rises upwards it shows that the individual is entering a period where she will be consciously controlling her emotions, that is, letting her head rule her heart (Figure 176a). This often happens if a person has been terribly hurt emotionally, perhaps after the break-up of an important relationship, for instance. If, however, the line should descend at any time in its course, it tells of a broadening of one's awareness, of an expansion of mind or an increase in the subject's creative and imaginative mental abilities (Figure 176b).

Any break which is overlapped by a new section of line reveals a complete change of orientation, a time when the individual comes to terms with herself, questions her beliefs and philosophy in life and re-formulates her aims and ambitions for the future. The actual process of change may be quite turbulent for some and may result in personal confusion and a temporary loss of direction. But once the process is complete, it will lead to a feeling almost of rebirth, of turning over a completely new leaf. The whole process, however, may take some time and it can be measured against the length of line which is overlapped. Whether the new section begins above or below the old gives important clues to the new trend of thought: higher up suggests a tougher approach (Figure 177a), and lower down indicates a softening or mellowing which brings with it greater understanding and more relaxation of mind (Figure 177b). A complete break is rare and when found may suggest an injury to the head (Figure 177c).

A change of direction is not often seen in the life line but when found the line usually sweeps outwards towards the centre of the palm. This formation reveals a broadening of the lifestyle, an expansion of one's horizons, a much wider environment than ever before. Often, when a break is seen here it is usually really an overlap where a new section of line begins a little way further towards the centre and the two are joined by a very fine hair line (Figure 178). This reveals a new life, perhaps a new start in a different country, or a marriage or career

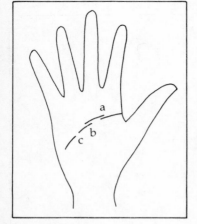

Figure 177

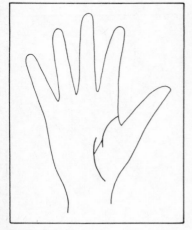

Figure 178

move which takes the individual into brand new environments and, again, a wider, more exciting way of life. If the new section of line happens to start inside the old, that is, towards the thumb, it indicates a closing up of the lifestyle with restrictions and limitations being imposed. An example of this might occur if an individual, accustomed to a life of luxury, were to suddenly find herself bankrupt and forced to eke out a meagre existence for the rest of her life. If a complete break does occur, and this is fairly rare, it can denote a sudden injury. If that break is covered by four little lines in a square formation it reveals that the individual is protected in some way and will recover from her misadventure.

BRANCHES

With just a very few exceptions, branches are almost always positive markings to possess. On the head line branches may be seen at any point shooting upwards towards the fingers and these reveal a sense of mental achievement. If one should travel up towards the index it denotes academic or scholastic success. In the direction of the middle finger it is connected with the realization of ambitions within one's career. A branch rising towards the ring finger tells of fulfilment and creative satisfaction. And one shooting up towards the little finger reveals business, scientific or financial success.

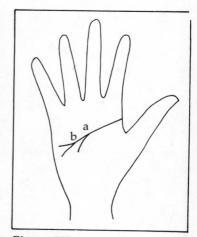

Figure 179

There are two strong branches splitting off the head line which are not event markings. One occurs directly below the ring finger and is known as the 'writer's fork' and as such denotes an abundance of creative, if not literary, powers (Figure 179a). The other, splitting off the head line beneath the little finger, shows business acumen and a good head for going into business on one's own (Figure 179b). But any tiny branches which are seen sprouting downwards, especially if they spring from a dip in the head line, are indeed event markings to look out for – these are the exceptional ones because they are not positive markings at all and, in fact, often denote a time of depression.

Any branches rising upwards from the life line are,

like those of the head line, positive indications of personal success. One to the index finger again highlights academic achievements. One towards the middle finger may either be interpreted as career advancement but more often indicates the successful outcome of property negotiations – such as the purchase of a first house, for example. A branch towards the ring finger shows contentment and satisfaction, and one shooting off in the direction of the little finger tells of personal, financial or business success.

Branches which shoot downwards, though, towards the Luna mount are signs of movement for they predict the likelihood of moves or travel or journeys. The longer they are and the further they penetrate into the mount of Luna, the farther the journey, which is often one in some way connected with water, such as a trip overseas. Short little branches often suggest an important change of address.

As the fate line normally terminates on the Saturn mount, a branch off this line would not usually be seen in that direction. But one which travels towards the index mount would certainly be interesting because this area could suggest public recognition and acclaim. Here, such a branch would highlight any achievements in the field of either politics, religion or the law. One that rises up towards the middle finger would signify a sense of creative fulfilment in one's work. And a branch towards the little finger would denote material prosperity, financial rewards, scientific or business success.

Branches are often seen rising from the percussion edge upwards to meet the fate line. When this occurs it is a wonderful indication of marriage or, in other words, of the beginning of a stable relationship (Figure 180a). Alas, if the branch either fails to meet the main fate line (Figure 180b), or crosses right over it (Figure 180c), this does not bode well as both of these indicate that the relationship will fail.

In the old palmistry tradition it has been said that branches which drop down from the heart line denote emotional disappointments. However, much more modern research needs to be carried out before these claims can be validated. Branches which rise

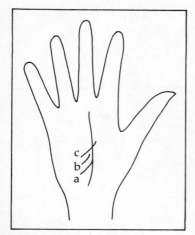

Figure 180

upwards from the heart line are rare but if found follow the same rules as those from the head and life lines except that the achievements would stem from a feeling of emotional success.

All the indications illustrated above can easily be dated using the time gauges described in Chapter 4 for the head line and Chapter 5 for the life and fate lines. In this way every individual can be prepared for any eventuality that is marked on the hand.

If it is an indication of a positive event then one could approach the prospect with greater confidence and peace of mind, and so in the process may be able to relish it that much more. Perhaps, too, being aware of the proposed success might mean one could approach it with a better frame of mind and bring more impact to bear, thus enhancing the whole situation.

When the signs are negative, one should not feel fatalistically propelled towards irrevocably detrimental events for such markings are mere indications and there is much that one can do before the events ever occur. Firstly, given prior knowledge, it could be possible to intervene and take preventive measures to ensure that the events never happen. Secondly, if an individual feels that the events are, in fact, unavoidable, at least she is prepared for them and can approach them with a stronger attitude of mind. Or thirdly, she could watch the signs and simply dodge around the circumstances surrounding the events and thereby lessen their impact.

In these ways we begin to gain control and mastery over our environment so that, instead of living our lives in the dark, afraid and unaware of our future, we can begin to look forward with happiness and confidence, to make the very best of each one of our gifts and talents and to choose for ourselves, at every turn, the direction we wish our lives to take.

APPENDIX
HOW TO TAKE
PRINTS

In order to take a clear and accurate hand print one does not necessarily require a great deal of expensive or elaborate equipment. In fact, people often send me prints which they have taken most successfully just by applying lipstick, and some even use boot polish.

So perhaps in the early stages, before spending time and money, I would recommend that anyone wanting to take a print should experiment at first with lipstick or shoe polish, either of which are usually readily available in most people's homes.

For a more professional finish, I list below my equipment and the method that I use:

Equipment

1. Ink roller
2. Sheet of glass (tile/formica square/etc.)
3. Tube of block printing ink (water-soluble)
4. Paper
5. Table knife
6. Tissues/cotton wool
7. Pencil

Method

Squeeze out $\frac{3}{8}$in (1cm) of ink onto glass or sheet of formica/tile/glossy paper and spread thinly with the roller. Using the roller, spread the ink over the hand, covering about 1in (3cm) of wrist, over the percussion edge and right to the tips of each digit. Shake hand and place in a comfortable or natural position on a sheet of paper. Trace outline with pencil and slip knife under paper, pressing it up into the hollow of the palm. Lift off and, if the print is too faint, has missing patches or too much ink, then just try again until a satisfactory impression has been taken.

If, as sometimes happens, the palm is so hollow that it simply refuses to print then there are several tricks which can be tried. One is to make a little mound out of tissues or cotton wool under the paper and to cup the hand over it. Another is to place the hand on the table, palm side up, lay the paper on top of it and gently press over the hand and into the hollow.

Always remember to write the individual's name, date of birth and whether they are right- or left-handed somewhere on the paper and, *most importantly*, the date on which the print was taken.

By using water-soluble block printing ink, the hands can then simply be washed with soap and water.

INDEX

INDEX